ACCESSIBLE LEARNING SPACES

A Guide to Implementing
UNIVERSAL DESIGN
in Early Childhood

CINDY MUDROCH, MEd

www.gryphonhouse.com

Copyright

Bulk Purchase

Gryphon House books are available for special premiums and sales promotions as well as for fund-raising use. Special editions or book excerpts also can be created to specifications. For details, call 800.638.0928.

Disclaimer

Gryphon House, Inc., cannot be held responsible for damage, mishap, or injury incurred during the use of or because of activities in this book. Appropriate and reasonable caution and adult supervision of children involved in activities and corresponding to the age and capability of each child involved are recommended at all times. Do not leave children unattended at any time. Observe safety and caution at all times.

DEDICATION

*This book is dedicated to my son, Robbie,
who was brilliant, funny, compassionate,
and positive his entire life.*

TABLE OF CONTENTS

INTRODUCTION

Since 1983, I have taught preschool through third grade as a general- and special-education teacher. I have always believed in making education accessible to all children. This belief became more personal with the birth of our third child, Robbie.

With our first two children, I never worried about their being included or receiving what they needed at school. When Robbie was born, everything changed. He started having ear infections at a few weeks old and experienced significant speech and language delays due to hearing problems. We immediately started interventions with a speech teacher, who came to our house twice a week to work with him. Adding to his difficulties, he also had significant sensory issues; he would not eat anything too hot or too cold. Thankfully, Robbie attended an outstanding early childhood program that used many universal design for learning (UDL) guidelines while providing a full-inclusion preschool program. They also incorporated the Reggio approach, an early childhood teaching philosophy that allows children to explore and learn while doing hands-on projects and that encourages visual and written documentation of children's engaged learning. His teachers used multiple means of instruction, so my son and other children who did not learn auditorily could understand the same lesson visually. Children who learned better kinesthetically were encouraged to touch, feel, and explore. Robbie went from being almost nonverbal and following very few directions to almost catching up to his peers with his language skills by age six. He was also showing usual math abilities; on an assessment, he scored at the 99th percentile for his age.

As he grew, Robbie faced challenges with his health. At age five, he was diagnosed with attention-deficit hyperactivity disorder (ADHD). He was thirteen years old when he was diagnosed with Asperger's syndrome, which is now included as part of autism spectrum disorder (ASD). At age fourteen, he was diagnosed with Marfan syndrome, a genetic connective-tissue disorder that affected his heart, lungs, and spine. He didn't let these barriers stop him. In high school, he attended the Oklahoma School of Science and Math for gifted children. He later graduated from the University of Tulsa with a computer science and mathematics degree. He is an early childhood UDL success story!

I firmly believe that all the interventions Robbie received as a young child opened the doors to his future success. Sadly, he was diagnosed with bone cancer at age twenty-one. While fighting the disease, he didn't give up on following his dreams. He had always wanted to work at Google, so he applied and they asked to interview him in person. Despite the fact that Robbie was by then physically disabled due to cancer, he flew to San Francisco. He was offered the job and a contract a few months later, but by then, his cancer was spreading quickly. A few days before he passed away, he asked me if I would write his story. As a mother and an educator, I am on a mission to spread the importance of the UDL mindset in the classroom.

Universal design frequently opens doors beyond the original purpose. What you change for a few people often benefits many more. For example, wheelchair ramps also benefit mothers with strollers, people walking pets, those who use walkers or canes, people carrying groceries or pulling luggage, children on scooters, the elderly, and many more. Consider the following inventions that were created for a specific audience but are now widely used by many.

- The keyboard was developed to help people who could not see to write by hand (History Computer Staff, 2021).

- The electric toothbrush was invented to help people with limited strength and mobility independently brush their teeth (Lee, 2009).

- The Foundation for the Blind first started using audiobooks in 1932 (Conn-Powers, Cross, Traub, and Hutter-Pishgahi, 2006). Now, these books are widely used by people of a variety of abilities.

These are notable examples of how an accommodation can benefit more than the intended population. The same idea applies to classrooms; flexible accommodations introduced for a few can benefit many more children.

How This Book Is Organized

Universal design for learning is not a special-education program—it is for all learners. All children benefit from having engaging lessons and more choices during the learning process. The UDL teaching method looks at the many needs of children and provides multiple pathways toward student success.

Chapter 1 introduces UDL and explains how the approach opens a new world with unlimited possibilities in the classroom. With UDL, schools can adjust learning materials, learning tools, and lesson plans to reach a broader range of abilities and needs. Educators can transform their classrooms from a traditional model to a model that provides equitable and accessible education for all.

In chapter 2, we delve deeper into the UDL guidelines and the fundamental principles they are founded on.

In chapter 3, we explore flipping the learning environment, examining ways to add more versatile choices while engaging children in discovery, exploration, and reaching their learning goals. When setting up a learning environment, many considerations support diverse teaching and learning. For example, educators can include innovative learning spaces that serve multiple functions and allow various means of instruction and learning. Flexible seating options can be helpful with focus, attention, and comfort.

Chapter 4 examines common learning variabilities and ways to help students succeed. *Learning variabilities* is a term that encompasses the many ways in which a disability, environment, disease, or genetic disorder could affect a child's ability to learn. But UDL is not limited to looking at learning disabilities; this method looks at the whole child. Children do not need a label or diagnosis for early interventions to start. For example, a child could be very bright, full of energy, and have trouble staying focused. Another child could come to school hungry, therefore lacking energy to keep up with her peers. UDL approaches make learning more flexible and accessible for all children.

In chapter 5, we look at ways to use low-, medium-, and high-tech interventions during instruction, learning, and assessment. Low-tech interventions include items such as pencil grips, different writing instruments, visuals, and non-electronic aids. A medium-tech example could be a unique seat cushion or weighted lap pad. High-tech examples include tablets such as iPads, computers, special adaptive equipment, and more.

Chapter 6 offers the reader ways to rethink lesson planning with UDL guidelines in mind. By looking at the classroom environment, learning variabilities, and technical interventions, along with the knowledge of UDL, teachers can plan for a broader range of students. Daily, children are expected to learn the same way as their peers.

The appendices explore inexpensive ideas for DIY projects for UDL classrooms, technology options to try, books for children with different learning variabilities, and further reading for educators.

As educators push for innovations and additional pathways for learning, they are on the front lines of education reform. As you begin or continue your UDL journey, remember my son Robbie, who faced many barriers in his short life, but he never gave up. His life story is the inspiration behind writing this book.

CHAPTER 1
Smart from the Start: An Introduction to Universal Design for Learning

"Do not confine your children to your learning, for they were born in another time."
• **Hebrew Proverb** •

Eli's Story

Several years ago, when I was teaching kindergarten, one family passed a sealed letter to me as they walked toward the door. I had just met their son, Eli, at kindergarten roundup and had talked with them for the first time. I started reading as they practically ran down the hallway and out of the school. Their letter shared more about their son and some of his problems. They did not know what was wrong, only that his preschool experience had left them afraid for him, and they were visibly scared to send him to kindergarten.

Eli had not fit the average expectations for a preschooler, where the curriculum included fingerpainting and playing nicely with friends. To avoid getting his hands dirty, he refused to fingerpaint or touch anything messy, and he frequently landed in time-out for being uncooperative. His playtime was also a disaster, as his social skills were significantly delayed. He was content playing by himself and twirling objects, and he would not think twice about taking an interesting toy from someone else. At an early age, he was becoming depressed from the daily failure to meet expectations.

Before the first day of kindergarten, I put a few supports into place for all the children. One change was to allow any child to use disposable gloves in the art center. This choice allowed Eli and other children to explore and learn without the sensory effect of messy hands. Eli smiled when he realized that he could fingerpaint and keep his hands clean.

Weeks later, when one glove slipped and his finger got wet, he realized he was okay. His face shined as he stuck both hands into the paint without gloves for the first time. His mother cried when she saw the picture of him fingerpainting without gloves.

Years later, when tested, Eli was found to be highly gifted and on the autism spectrum. Early childhood barriers had often kept him from showing his full potential. Eli's story is one of the many reasons I am passionate about using the strategies and philosophies behind universal design for learning. UDL methods do not have to be significant changes to have a significant impact on children's lives.

What Is Universal Design for Learning?

Imagine that you can shop for groceries only in your age group's most common store areas. But if you need gluten-free, lactose-free, or specialty foods, you must wait and have someone take you and your group to a separate room for your groceries. If your food needs are too great, they will not let you in the regular grocery store at all. You can see other people coming and going, but you are left out. It is a widespread practice in education to provide materials, instruction, and assessment for the typical child. Many children, including dual language learners and children with learning disabilities or giftedness, are left out.

The philosophy behind this method is much more than another teaching strategy that the next education fad will replace. It is a mindset that all children deserve and benefit from equal rights to an education free of barriers and separation from their peers. Yes, there is still a place and need for specialized programs, but a more inclusive education is possible within a UDL classroom. Children have the right to access what they need to succeed without waiting to fail or waiting for a unique program to allow them what they need.

Universal design for learning is a mindset that looks at planning smart from the start by examining potential learning barriers and considering ways to make learning more accessible to all students. Instead of traditional methods that often leave many children underserved and underachieving, "UDL is flexible and based on the premise that there is no 'one size fits all'" (Thoma, Bartholomew, and Scott 2009). UDL involves incorporating variabilities that benefit all children into the original design of learning materials, assistive technology, computer programs, buildings, and accommodations. This method allows children to use the same learning materials with innovative designs from the start. For example, adding a graphic organizer to a textbook chapter to help students organize the main ideas is a UDL method. Even a simple change, such as gloves for fingerpainting, can make a difference for a child. The UDL guidelines are used in settings for people of all ages, from preschools to universities, as educators plan for all students to become expert learners.

Flexibility and choice are often missing in education. Everyone, not just children with identified learning challenges, has unique needs. Teachers also have limits placed on them and are frequently restricted to using a one-size-fits-all curriculum that limits their gifts and individuality. A traditional classroom or school often examines student data and does not consider obstacles as a reason for assessment scores to fall below expectations.

Some obstacles that children face can, in fact, impact their learning. For example, when a child struggles with hearing and the instruction lacks visuals, that child is at a disadvantage in learning the lesson. Inflexibility can also cause children to be excluded. For example, if a teacher restricts children to answering questions verbally, a child who has limited language skills may struggle to show what they know. That child may be great at numbers but doesn't respond to the teacher's questions. The teacher may assume the child does not know the answers. On the other hand, if the teacher offers the children multiple ways to show what they know, that same child can draw or point to numbers. A true measure of the child's ability is possible.

Focus is another challenge for some children. They may miss instructions or directions and end up being lost when the rest of the class starts a project or lesson. I have seen an entire class line up, but the easily distracted child has no idea why the class is leaving and becomes distressed. A child with sensory sensitivities may struggle to concentrate on class activities. The lighting or noise in the room could affect their performance.

A child with undiagnosed vision issues can have a hard time learning. A child who processes information more slowly than their peers may give up during an assessment because they become overwhelmed. If the teacher changes the assessment by breaking it down to only a few questions at a time, the same child can excel.

Unfortunately, educators often accept the outcomes as the best the children can do, without considering each child's learning variabilities. With high accountability and the expectation that all children will master both general and specialized curricula, educators are looking for strategies to help students thrive. The need for better-designed instruction, materials, and classrooms is a top priority. Once you dive into the UDL approach, you will realize that everyone benefits from a more flexible mindset. Educators with choices, flexibility, and support can help their students excel. More students can demonstrate their knowledge without the many barriers commonly faced to receiving an equitable and accessible education.

What if educators offered a wide range of choices during the planning, learning, and assessing process? What if educators set up the learning environment to make the essential concepts accessible to everyone? The core value of UDL is to design education for all. "UDL is about taking your skill, your passion, and your craft and designing your lessons with embedded options, so they are relevant, accessible, and challenging to all students" (Novak, 2016).

UDL is "a scientifically valid instructional framework for guiding the design of learning environments that support all students" (Zhang et al., 2021). UDL methods mean considering learning variability during initial planning. Research has shown that the problem lies not in the student but in the barriers created by the curriculum and learning environment (Hitchcock, Meyer, Rose, and Jackson, 2002). All students benefit from having multiple means of learning available that allow them to show their full potential. UDL creates a learning atmosphere that is accessible and equitable for all.

Often, UDL is misunderstood as useful only for children in special education, but flexibility in learning using the latest brain research is what all children need. UDL takes excellent teaching to a higher level by adjusting existing curricula and materials for multiple levels of learning and additional flexibility. It is not expensive to add more choices and flexibility to education, but the rewards for the students are priceless.

The Research behind UDL

The rigor behind the UDL guidelines comes from evidence gained through years of research. UDL transforms education from the start with smart planning that incorporates a balance of support and challenges. It is not about making learning easier but about reducing unnecessary barriers to learning while continuing to work toward helping all children become expert learners. Instead of looking at the learners as the problem, the focus is on inflexible goals, materials, methods, and assessments (Hall, Meyer, and Rose, 2012). The guidelines are a significant shift from traditional education, which tries to fit the child to the curriculum rather than create a curriculum to meet children's needs.

UDL does not stop with lesson planning; this method looks at print accommodations; low, medium, and high tech; flexible seating; accessible environments; and behavior management. Advances in neuroscience have changed our understanding of how the brain works. "The notion of broad categories of learners as 'smart–not smart,' 'disabled–not disabled,' 'regular–not regular' is a gross over simplification that does not reflect reality" (Hall, Meyer, and Rose, 2012). Instead, a child's ability is not static but constantly changing and interacting with their environment. The results of brain research show that the "average" student does not exist (Hall, Meyer, and Rose, 2012). "The concept of neuro-variability is important for educators because it reminds us that learners do not have an isolated learning 'style,' but instead rely on many parts of the brain working together to function within a given context" (CAST, 2018b).

The UDL concept started many years ago with Ronald Mace. He contracted polio at age nine and from then on, he set out to remove barriers that he found everywhere. He became an advocate for accessibility and was one of the people behind the Fair Housing Amendments and Americans with Disabilities Act of 1990 (Bowe, 2000). The act addressed the rights and needs of those with disabilities and prohibited discrimination based on disability in jobs, government programs, public transportation, stores, parks, and so on. A person using a wheelchair is no longer excluded from public buildings and job opportunities (Thornburgh and Fine, 2000). After signing this act, George W. Bush said, "Let the shameful walls of exclusion come tumbling down" (Thornburgh and Fine, 2000). Students in wheelchairs who couldn't attend their neighborhood school, library, church, or store would finally be able to go without the challenge of barriers.

Ron Mace worked for the Center for Accessible Housing at North Carolina State University (NCSU), which was later called the Center for Universal Design. He pioneered the early work in UDL. "Ron Mace provided national leadership on accessibility" (Bowe, 2000). As an architect, Mace showed that putting universal design into the original building construction was cheaper and allowed for better accessibility than the costly additions required later to make buildings accessible. What started as a design for buildings has become the framework for accessible education (Bowe, 2000).

Another organization, the Center for Applied Special Technology (CAST), supports and researches UDL. The CAST approach is that designing more flexible learning environments will result in more effective learning. For example, developing and using technology to help children who are struggling to learn to read can also benefit other students. Interactive textbooks designed for children with special needs also offer learning opportunities that general-education students can use (O'Neill and Dalton, 2002).

UDL is recommended by the Every Student Succeeds Act (ESSA) of 2015, which replaced the No Child Left Behind Act. With further brain research, UDL will continue to evolve to meet changing educational needs.

How UDL Looks in the Classroom

Every child has a profile of strengths and weaknesses. UDL uses that profile to adjust instruction and assessment to bring out a child's strengths by putting in place accommodations and modifications that give the child what they need to succeed. For example, a child who is very active could have a wiggle seat or weighted lap pad during circle time or work time to help him focus. He might not have any specific diagnosis, but by noticing a need and putting in place a plan to help the child, the educator is naturally utilizing the UDL method. Very simply, when an educator is flexible and puts into place what children need when they need it, more students will be successful.

> In observing a school with pre-K through third-grade classrooms, I saw the teachers guiding children toward their learning goals and expectations, I saw the children actively involved with highly motivating lessons. Very few children sat at tables or desks. Instead, they moved around, building vocabulary and exploring different materials or carrying a clipboard with paper attached for writing. The UDL guideline of multiple means of representation was evident in every classroom.
>
> I did not observe children being left out because of the different skill levels. The teachers implemented scaffolding and assistive technology so children could learn side by side. For example, a teacher had additional small visuals on a ring that she used to cue some students. Other accommodations included wiggle seats and other types of

seating. Some areas offered various kinds of lighting rather than bright fluorescent lights.

The children knew the teachers' expectations during the learning process. Visual schedules helped them understand what activities were happening when, and children used nonverbal signs to communicate everyday needs, such as using the bathroom. Teachers had transition routines, and the children knew exactly where to go next. One teacher sang the start of a song when it was time to line up or clean up and move to the next area or activity. Another teacher had a little chime light she lightly hit, and the musical sounds let the children know what was next.

I observed they had adapted storybooks, so children who needed more visuals had that support. Other children could enjoy the added pictures. It was evident that teachers used multiple representations to present the learning objectives. The teachers ensured the children could interact and show what they had learned in various ways. Best of all, there was a high level of student engagement and motivation for learning.

With the UDL mindset, children can flourish and have the opportunity to reach their potential without limitations. Every child has different learning variabilities. All children come to school with their own backgrounds and prior knowledge, making all learners unique.

UDL in a High-Poverty School

Children in schools with a higher poverty level have challenges that other schools might not experience as often. These children may require different methods for student success. Challenges can include a lack of exposure to books, music, and arts. The children may never have traveled beyond their own neighborhoods. Some children may come to school hungry or in need of medical care. Behavioral concerns may be higher because children are struggling to navigate at school when their world outside of school is dramatically different. They may not have high trust in adults and will perform better in a school that recognizes this and allows for more student choices and flexibility. If children have experienced trauma, their brains might easily jump into a "fight or flight mode" if they perceive a threat. Consequently, educators should be ready to adjust their teaching style and methods to fit the needs of their students and to help the children to feel more connected to the school and learning.

By incorporating UDL principles with multiple means of engagement, representation, and expression, children have more opportunities to engage in learning. Following is a success story of how a high-poverty school was turned around by a shift in mindset from a traditional model to the UDL model.

> The school, located in a poverty-stricken neighborhood, had many students with significant learning needs and challenging behavior. Behavior-incident rates were higher than those in areas with less poverty, and test scores for a large percentage of the children were well below state norms. Sixty percent of the families served lived at or below the poverty line. Some of the families struggled to provide for basic needs, such as food and medical care. Residents of the neighborhood faced a higher incidence of drugs, prostitution, and crime. Adults in the neighborhood had a low rate of literacy, which made it hard for them to support their children's learning. For the most part, most families were doing the best they could for their children, but many lacked the skills or money to meet the children's everyday needs. These circumstances affected the children's ability to learn. If they were hungry or worried about not having supper later, the children would struggle to focus at school. If children had poor role models of acceptable behavior, they might act out at school because that was what they saw or heard at home. This background set the stage for a school facing lots of challenges.

> A talented principal had the vision to change the school by implementing the Reggio approach along with many UDL guidelines. Reggio includes project learning and the rigor of state standards, data,

and documentation (Tijnagel-Schoenaker, 2018). UDL blends well with the Reggio approach because both of these methods value the child as worthy, strong, active, and inquisitive about the world.

Teachers and staff participated in professional development and then slowly transitioned the school by changing how they planned and engaged in teaching. Teachers used highly motivating lessons and offered many choices for exploring and expression during learning, including student-directed learning, the arts, and projects. Teachers used assessment, documentation, high expectations, and data to guide their classroom decisions. The children had opportunities to communicate and represent themselves through both traditional and non-traditional academic modalities. They could engage in dance, drama, music, and creative art and were encouraged to celebrate learning beyond the typical classroom academics.

The results were impressive, with fewer office referrals and absent children, more engagement during lessons, and increased test scores. Some students had excelled and thrived before the changes, but many children had faced barriers too significant to allow them to show their potential. Observing classrooms with all the children engaged in learning was genuinely remarkable.

CHAPTER 2
The UDL Guidelines and Fundamental Principles

"If the child is not learning the way you are teaching, then you must teach in the way the child learns."

• Rita Dunn, researcher and educator •

Universal Design for Learning Guidelines support using scientific insights into how humans learn to maximize teaching and learning. The goal is for students to become expert learners who are purposeful and motivated, resourceful, knowledgeable, strategic, and goal directed (CAST, 2022b).

Brain-Based Teaching and Learning

UDL considers how the brain works, the many variabilities among students, and even those within each student. The UDL guidelines are a list of recommendations to aid the teacher in reducing barriers and optimizing learning. They can be mixed and matched to address specific learning goals and implemented into various subject areas (CAST, 2022b). Lesson planning that allows for more learning pathways to reach the target goal opens the doors to unlimited learning.

David Rose is a cofounder of CAST, a research and development organization working to enhance education for all learners through the UDL methods. He is a neuropsychologist with a background in education who has taught learners in preschool through graduate school. His work has largely focused on the development of innovative technologies for education to help improve learning for every child. By knowing how the brain works, educators can use that knowledge to engage more children in effective learning. The three main areas of the brain that Rose connects to learning are affective, recognition, and strategic networks (CAST, 2022b).

Affective Networks

Affective networks of the brain regulate emotions and processing, enabling learners to engage in learning. The UDL guideline of using multiple means of engagement is connected to the affective networks, which help children get excited about and engaged in learning. For example, a preschool teacher uses a weather-bear puppet during circle time to get the children excited about the weather. The teacher also has a weather song that the children sing, and then she reads a weather story. By engaging the children using high-interest methods, she will gain their attention and focus.

Reflective Networks

The recognition networks involve gathering and sorting information, which help students to identify and understand concepts when the educator uses multiple methods for teaching the information. Returning to our preschool weather lesson, weather is a big topic, so the teacher plans lessons across several days and circle times and varies the methods of instruction. One day, the teacher will use the weather bear, the song, and the story. The next day, she might use the smartboard to engage the children by allowing them to interact with the board and move around the correct weather pictures for the day. Another day, she might take the children and the weather bear outside to decide on the weather and make drawings of what they learn using a simple visual graphic organizer and a clipboard. They can discuss what the bear should wear and then dress the bear for going outdoors.

Strategic Networks

Strategic networks connect with the UDL guideline of action and expression, which help the student with planning and self-monitoring. Students can show what they know in different ways that work best for their learning styles. For example, after the teacher has taught her weather unit for a few days, she may have the children show what they know about the weather vocabulary by drawing clouds, sun, rain, and snow. They might orally tell the teacher or point to visuals. A few might even start using inventive spelling by putting letters with their pictures. By allowing different methods to show what they know, a greater number of children will have a chance to be successful.

UDL Guidelines and Checkpoints

The UDL Guidelines (CAST, 2022b), available online at https://udlguidelines. cast.org, offer many strategic ways to effectively teach a wide range of students. Reviewing all the guidelines might seem overwhelming, but remember that even a slight change can have a considerable impact. Many teachers are naturally incorporating many of the guidelines into their classrooms. The guidelines are not intended as a to-do list. Use them to transform your classroom approaches from traditional methods aimed at the average student to a broader spectrum of learning without limits.

Affective Networks of the Brain: The "Why" of Learning

Provide multiple means of engagement. The key idea is to engage students using multiple methods, allowing for a wide range of learning variabilities within the classroom. For example, let's say that a teacher is creating a lesson on a math concept. For children who respond well to visual and interactive learning, the teacher can use the smartboard with the lesson and invite children to touch the correct number, set, or answer. For children who prefer auditory learning, short video clips can explain the concept and reinforce their understanding. Children who learn best through tactile experiences can engage with the concept using manipulatives.

Provide options for recruiting interest: Children will not learn what they do not pay attention to. To spark their interest, teachers can offer an intriguing attention grabber. For example, showing a short video clip of a whale before reading a book or having a lesson about a whale may capture the children's attention. Another example is using a puppet to help read a story or offering a mystery box that children can reach into, touch an object related to the next topic, and try to guess what it is.

- **Optimize individual choice and autonomy:** Allowing students to have options while exploring and learning makes them feel more invested in their education and builds independence and self-confidence. Teachers do need to decide in advance which choices will enhance learning (Parker, Novak, and Bartell, 2017). There are many ways to add choices into a child's school day to help them to feel more a part of the learning process. For example, consider letting children pick where they sit, choose a partner to work or explore learning with, or select what to do first from among a few choices. Children can pick whether they want blue paper or green paper, crayons or markers, being with a group or going to a quiet spot in the room, standing up while working or sitting in a chair—the list goes on. Having choices helps with confidence, which is evident when a child realizes they can make decisions throughout their day. Allowing choices increases student engagement, because they become excited when they can make decisions about what they are going to do or how they are going to do it. They have to problem solve and make decisions. Freedom to choose for themselves builds more independence because they are not relying on someone to tell them explicitly what to do for every step.

- **Optimize relevance, value, and authenticity:** Having authentic and relevant instruction helps build connections with prior learning. Authentic learning is a type of teaching that encourages children to make relationships between experiences and new learning. They can explore and expand their knowledge and feel ownership in learning as active participants. Some examples include acting out a familiar story, writing to an author, setting up a store to work on money skills, dressing up as community helpers, planting a garden in science, hatching eggs into chicks while learning about life cycles, taking care of a class pet to work on responsibility, cooking while incorporating math and language skills. There are endless ways to incorporate real-life experiences and problems into learning, which helps children to make connections in their brain to the new learning (AWE Learning, 2016).

- **Minimize threats and distractions:** A structured environment where children feel safe and free from chaos will allow them to feel safe enough to learn. Loud and threatening teachers cause children to spend more time worrying than learning. It is best to have a positive classroom-management plan.

- **Provide options for sustaining effort and persistence:** Engaged students can maintain focus and sustain effort longer. For example, if a class is learning about volcanoes and the teacher has an experiment demonstrating a volcano in action, children are more likely to remain focused. If, on the other hand, the teacher simply verbally explains about a volcano, children's interest may quickly fade.

- **Heighten salience of goals and objectives:** You may need prompts and visuals or need to explain the goals and objectives in diverse ways. Some children may need reminding of what the goal of the lesson is. If a lesson or project has multiple steps, help the children break it into manageable parts to help them stay engaged during the learning process.

- **Vary demands and resources to optimize the challenge:** Children differ in the challenges they respond to. When learning, vary the degree of difficulty, share separate ways students could be challenged, or adjust as needed to support individual learners. For example, some children could count sets with manipulatives in a math lesson, and others could work on adding or subtracting. In contrast, another group of students could make numbers out of playdough to develop number recognition. All can be happening simultaneously on diverse levels, with everyone learning with their peers and moving toward the goals and objectives set up for the lesson.

- **Foster collaboration and community:** Encourage children to cheer each other on to success. Use community-building activities, such as a community circle or circle time, depending on the age, so the children get to know each other better and feel a part of the group. Another way is to have children work in groups on a specific project or activity with teacher guidance. One school where I worked had fun, child-friendly chants with motions that they could do together to cheer on another classmate. The look on a child's face when the entire class cheers for them is priceless.

- **Increase mastery-oriented feedback:** Assessment and feedback are an essential part of learning. Children learn best when they have feedback that is as immediate as possible, specific, and positive. For example, when a young child is first learning letter sounds, the immediate teacher feedback will help the child know whether the sound they are producing is correct, which avoids practicing a skill incorrectly. The teacher could repeat the sound and say, for example, "Great job saying the short *A* sound correctly." After a learning assessment, when a teacher gives feedback that is specific, the children can learn from areas that they struggled with and continue to grow in areas where they had success. Specific positive feedback is important as a motivator for children when they are learning. I have noticed when I teach that children are excited to learn and try new things because they know, whether they miss a question or arrive at the correct answer, I will be positive and help them toward success.

- **Provide options for self-regulation:** Children do not automatically know what to do when they experience big emotions or choices. As part of their classroom management plan, teachers can show children ways to help them to self-regulate their emotions and learning.

- **Promote expectations and beliefs that optimize motivation:** *Motivation* is defined as the engagement process between the student and the learning environment, which increases their interest and helps them be determined to work toward the goal or skill being taught (Seel, Svinicki, and Vogler, 2012). For example, a teacher might use a puppet with a book during circle time to engage the children's interest and motivation in listening to the story. Another teacher might take the children on a virtual field trip related to the same topic they are currently studying, to increase their desire to learn more.

- **Facilitate personal coping skills and strategies:** Video clips, modeling, books, and lessons can help children understand that everyone has big feelings. Educators can also teach them how to use the sensory and quiet areas of the classroom to regroup. Students could have a break card they can give to the teacher when they feel overwhelmed. Some teachers offer acceptable choices of break activities on a menu board. Children do not usually abuse this practice because they like to stay with the group. Still, occasionally I have limited a child's choices, which is all part of the training they receive as they learn the classroom management plan.

- **Develop self-assessment and reflection:** Even the youngest student can go over a social story that gives a child-friendly narrative of what happened, how that made others feel, and options of what to do next time. They can learn how to reflect on their choice and what would be a better choice the next time.

Recognition Networks of the Brain: The "What" of Learning

Provide multiple means of representation. Children exhibit a broad range of learning variabilities. For example, a classroom could easily include students with visual issues, auditory processing problems, sensory sensitivities, attention and focus points, and a wide range of different experiences, making it difficult to reach all the children using traditional methods. By using UDL, the educator has a greater chance of reaching more students. For example, by pairing visuals with auditory and tactile experiences, the teacher can go from reaching a few children to having multiple children engaged.

Provide options for perception: Traditional classrooms are primarily verbal, so even very bright children who struggle with auditory processing or who cannot hold multiple directions in their minds at one time can end up behind the class. For example, if a teacher gives instructions to first wash hands and then have a snack, the child with auditory issues might only hear "have a snack" and then get in trouble for not following the other directions. With the simple modification of using visuals and posting visual steps for everyday events, the same child can quickly look at the visual order and independently follow the directions. Visuals are beneficial whenever a teacher needs children to get out specific items. By putting visuals up on the board or smartboard, the children can independently gather what is required. In addition, visuals help children who are learning English as a second language follow along with classroom activities. Visuals are a powerful tool.

- **Offer ways of customizing the display of information:** If you know you have a student with a visual impairment, then it's essential to consider the color and size of font and materials used. For example, higher contrast might be needed, such as black font on a white background, or the display may need to be adjusted. If a child has vision issues, the teacher can move her to be closer to instruction, whether it be a desk in the front or sitting by the teacher during circle time. When displaying information, clipart or actual photos may help the student understand the information being shared. The design and layout of anchor charts make a tremendous difference in how children understand the information being taught. For example, the anchor chart might show letters and pictures of things that start with the letter sounds. These charts are used by early childhood teachers as a visual way to convey information that has been taught. Teachers display them as references for the children. When the teacher displays them neatly, children can easily find the information.

- **Offer alternatives for auditory information:** Other options include visuals, tactile items, three-dimensional objects, or manipulatives.

- **Offer alternatives for visual information:** Some children prefer to hear information to process it, such as by using audiobooks, listening to videos, or using text-to-speech software.

Provide options for language and symbols: It is helpful to clarify vocabulary with visuals. Teachers can introduce symbols in several ways to help build understanding. For example, math concepts are often taught with manipulatives first, and later additional skills are introduced until students can master their goals. The same is true for other areas of learning. It sometimes takes a multisensory approach to bridge the gap in understanding a new concept. The following checkpoints are suggestions to use when teaching to avoid confusion.

- **Clarify vocabulary and symbols:** One method is to preteach vocabulary and symbols. For example, I show visuals and preteach vocabulary during a guided reading lesson. Visuals help children understand what they are reading or hearing. A teacher can guide younger children to look at pictures and discuss what might happen in the story and can clarify any new images or terms. Next, the teacher reads the story, allowing the children to have a higher level of understanding.

- **Clarify syntax and structure:** In math, children often need help understanding why the arrangement of a formula is important. Similarly, in reading, sentence structure makes a difference in meaning. Making connections to prior learning helps when clarifying syntax and structure. Ask children to explain what they think a word means, and then explain unfamiliar terms for a specific lesson as needed.

- **Support decoding of text, mathematical notation, and symbols:** As children advance through learning, they may need added scaffolding to learn how to decode symbols and notation. Knowing your students well and the type and amount of support they will need to succeed is essential.

- **Promote understanding across languages:** Promoting language across all cultures is essential because we are a multicultural society. Knowing your students will help you know if added support or visuals are needed. For example, children who are English learners or who use American Sign Language will need support in both their dominant language and English to help them understand terminology and information and also make connections.

- **Illustrate through multiple media:** Provide information and explain concepts through a variety of means, such as illustrations, diagrams, models, music, dance, images, video, play, and art.

- **Provide options for comprehension:** Processing and understanding information varies with each child in a classroom. Therefore, it is essential to provide options for comprehension. By using all the earlier guidelines with multiple means of engagement, representation, action, and expression, children will have many possibilities for understanding a concept or lesson.

- **Activate or supply background knowledge:** By activating background knowledge, teachers help children make connections in their brains. These connections make it easier to learn and recall the information later. Many teachers already use this method every day in their classrooms. For example, before reading and learning about space, a teacher might show the children video clips and pictures of planets. She might ask the children what they have noticed about the moon and help them connect new information about space with their prior knowledge. She might use models of the planets and solar system to support their understanding.

- **Highlight patterns, critical features, big ideas, and relationships:** Teachers can explain and show students text features, such as pictures and diagrams, to help explain a story or big ideas.

- **Guide information processing and visualization:** Help children visualize when they hear or read text. Help them understand connections and build understanding using models. Break big ideas into smaller groups or concepts to scaffold understanding. Cue steps with words such as *first*, *then*, *next*, and *finally*.

- **Maximize transfer and generalization:** Generalization is another reason students need to learn information through multiple modalities. The key to learning is transferring and using information in other places. Give children opportunities to experience a concept in many ways. If, for example, a child sees only the letter *A* on a sheet of blue paper, she might transfer that blue is the letter *A* and miss the point entirely. Recently some of my eight-year-old students with special needs took a science vocabulary test covering terms they had learned with accompanying visuals. When their teacher gave them the test without the visuals, they could not transfer and apply the information because the words alone did not have meaning for them.

Strategic Networks of the Brain: The "How" of Learning

Provide multiple means of action and expression. Children vary in the ways they can show what they know. They are highly creative, and if they know the information and are given a chance, educators can find ways to assess knowledge and gather data. One way to look at assessment is to think about the target goal as a destination on a map. Your instruction is like the different routes to get to the destination. How a child learns could depend on the route. Like some families, some children might need a few rest stops or to take a detour; other children will take the fastest route possible. They will all arrive at the goal but in diverse ways. Use a rubric of the steps completed to master the goal, which will give the educator data for assessing learning.

Provide options for physical action: Offer learning materials so that students can physically interact with success. For example, some children might access information with a printed book. Others might need to interact with a digital book or may benefit from page-turning help. Writing utensils might vary, depending on children's ages and abilities. Consider the classroom learning materials from the point of view of each child. Be sure to provide materials that each child can navigate.

- **Vary the methods for response and navigation:** Children vary in how they can navigate the physical classroom. It is best to design the classroom to meet the many needs of the students. As a special education teacher, I visit many different classrooms. Sometimes, they are set up with an average child in mind, and children who have difficulty with motor planning, vision, hearing, or sensory sensitivities are not considered. A child with sensory issues placed in a loud area of the classroom may fall apart due to the noise. Having limited space for classroom navigation may make it difficult for a student who struggles with motor planning to engage in some classroom areas. I have seen children stand frozen in place, unable to figure out how to go around other children or furniture in the classroom.

- **Optimize access to tools and assistive technologies:** Assistive technology and learning tools should be easily accessible to whoever needs them. Some assistive technology items include wiggle seats, weighted lap pads, special pencil grips, different types of writing utensils, noise-cancellation headphones, and many other possibilities, depending on the children and what helps them learn best. It is interesting to note that when an assistive technology tool is introduced, all the children want to try it out. Then after a while, I have noticed that children who need something will access it. How tools are introduced makes a difference. Assistive technology is not a special education tool; it is a tool for any child to use to help them to be successful. Some children like to accessorize and might not need a specific tool, but they enjoy utilizing the accommodations.

Provide options for expression and communication: Children need options for expressing themselves, especially in early childhood education when they are still learning language and communication skills. Children cannot always express what they know in words. Children with specific learning disabilities or language delays may also need other ways to express themselves. A nonverbal child is not a nonthinking child. People often assume that a child who needs options for communication is delayed academically. For example, my son could only speak a few words when he started the three-year-old early childhood program, but he could run all the electronics in our house. If the goal were to verbally explain how to turn on movies, music, or the microwave, he would have failed. But if you asked him to show you, he could. If a child struggles to communicate verbally, offer the options of drawing, pointing, and using assistive technology to show what they know or need. It may take time to create an assessment that meets the needs of a variety of children, but it also takes time to reteach skills because it appears a child has not mastered a goal. Smart planning saves time.

- **Use multiple media for communication:** Speech-to-text programs for writing may sound like they are for older children, but young children enjoy them too. They can speak into a Google doc, and it will type it for them. They can then use the text-to-speech feature, and the program will read it back to them. For children in elementary school who struggle to keep up with their peers, speech-to-text can be a huge help in expressing their ideas and understandings.

- **Use multiple tools for construction and composition:** Give children access to graphic organizers, both paper and digital; different writing utensils; sentence starters; spell checkers; and virtual or concrete manipulatives. They will be more likely to engage with learning and reach their goals when they feel supported in expressing their ideas.

- **Build fluencies with graduated levels of support for practice and performance:** Children build fluency as they learn to recognize shapes, numbers, and letters, then move on to reading and writing words and stories and understanding and expressing math facts. They need varying levels of support as they practice and learn. For example, when children are first learning how to hold a writing utensil, they might need hand-over-hand assistance along with verbal or visual prompts. The teacher will slowly reduce the amount of support as children's skills grow.

Provide options for executive functions: Children learn to self-monitor, set goals, and reflect on their progress as they grow and learn. Younger children will need more support to learn about self-monitoring and reflection. Invite children to set goals and help them take steps to reach them. Younger children can point to a picture to pick a goal, and older children can plan for short-term and long-term goals.

- **Guide appropriate goal setting:** Depending on the age of the children, provide goal ideas and examples. For example, preschool children might pick goals to work on for the day or week from among a small group of pictures. As children get older, they can pick academic or behavioral goals.

- **Support planning and strategy development:** This includes the scaffolding process of deciding steps for reaching goals. If a child struggles to stay with the group during circle time each day, she might choose that goal and earn a sticker to monitor her progress. Even the youngest child can be guided to set up a goal and track progress. Monitoring progress is part of becoming responsible for learning and supports the joy of accomplishment.

- **Facilitate managing information and resources:** When children need help with executive functions, managing the information and resources presented to them is difficult (CAST, 2022). Teachers can provide accommodations to help children hold or sort information in their minds to help them succeed. Even children with no problems in this area will benefit from these accommodations. For example, graphic organizers, checklists, breaking down the project or assignment into manageable steps, allowing for the information to be shared in different ways, number charts, and manipulatives help children organize and use information and resources.

- **Enhance capacity for monitoring progress:** Children can track progress in many ways. I have had children build a paper ice-cream cone with multiple paper scoops; they can add a scoop each time they meet their goal. Children might move a paper rocket up a sign, add stickers or stars to a chart, or add a little pompom to a jar. As children are able, they can color in bar graphs to track progress. Data graphs work well for fluency in numbers, letters, reading, and math. Students try harder when they can track their progress.

UDL embraces the latest brain research on how students learn, and the guidelines help teachers as they plan and teach using multiple means of engagement, representation, and action and expression. Integrating the UDL guidelines into the curriculum is part of working toward unlocking every student's potential by creating opportunities to learn through multiple modalities, explore in a stimulating environment, and show what they have learned without being limited to one path. Multiple learning pathways allow children to become expert learners without barriers and to be partners in their learning.

Accommodations and assistive technology help all children on their path to learning excellence. Traditional teaching methods often hold children back in a cocoon of defeat. Whether implemented in a classroom or an entire school, even a minor change can significantly improve student learning. A child is waiting for an educator with the vision to see their hidden potential while removing barriers allowing them to soar.

CHAPTER 3
Rethinking the Classroom Environment

....

*"Given a rich environment, learning
becomes like the air—it's in and around us."*
• Sandra Dodd (2019) •

I had ten years of experience teaching kindergarten in a private preschool and had always had excellent classroom control. But when I started teaching at a new school in a high-crime area of a city, I quickly learned how naïve I was. I had put together traditional lesson plans that were textbook perfect. Unfortunately, my second- and third-grade students faced barriers that I did not anticipate, and my first day was a disaster! By the end of the day, my students had poked each other with every possible school supply, had tossed desks, broken pencils, yelled, sworn, and had done zero classwork. What was missing? One problem was trust. I needed to build a relationship with them, and I needed to understand their learning barriers. These barriers were not limited to academic challenges. As I got to know my students better, I learned about some of the additional challenges they faced. Some had parents doing the best they could but who also had academic challenges, so the home environment was missing books or someone to read to them. Medical care was not readily available to all the children, so getting glasses or following up on hearing problems did not always happen. Some students lacked basic needs such as enough food and warm clothing. My classroom arrangement and teaching methods needed to adjust to the needs of my students. As an educator, I had to look beyond their scores and consider the whole child when planning. I scrapped my lesson plans, and I cleared my classroom with the help of an older janitor who felt sorry for me. We removed all the desks, and he helped me to put tables in the classroom instead. I locked up the classroom supplies that had not been destroyed, including all the textbooks.

When the students returned the next day, I had quiet music playing. We started over with new ideas and plans that better matched their needs. The first few weeks might have appeared to be a waste of time; we played educational games together, learned classroom expectations, used technology for writing, and learned math and reading by cooking. But the time was well spent because the biggest change was that they learned they could trust me. This allowed them to feel safe enough to learn. The more they trusted me, the more they were willing to do.

As the weeks went by, I added academics into our activities until eventually we were running an entire academic school day. It was a bumpy ride and never perfect, but by building relationships with the children, I was able to remove some of the barriers to their learning.

> **"CLASSROOMS DESIGNED TO HONOR CHILDREN ARE ENVIRONMENTS FILLED WITH CHOICES, MEANINGFUL EXPERIENCES, RESPECTFUL INTERACTIONS, COMMUNICATION, AND RELEVANT COLLABORATIONS."**
>
> —Sandra Duncan, Jody Martin, and Sally Haughey, *Through a Child's Eyes*

An engaging and stimulating environment supports children and their access to learning. In addition, a positive environment can help to strengthen a child's social-emotional growth.

What steps should educators take as they plan to implement UDL in their classrooms? Is it possible for classroom design to affect learning access for students? In this chapter, we explore steps educators can take to transform their classrooms into places where children can thrive. Remember: you don't have to do it all at once. It is okay to start small and not try to do it all.

Step 1: Understanding UDL as It Affects the Classroom Environment

The UDL approach to setting up a classroom is sort of like that of a hotel: Instead of waiting until the guests (children) arrive, the space is organized to allow all who come there to access everything that is offered. Accommodations are set up ahead of time, and signs and visuals make it easy for everyone to navigate and find what they need. The goal is to create a stimulating environment where guests (children) feel safe and comfortable and have the accommodations and modifications they need to take advantage of all the amenities.

> "A WELL-DESIGNED CLASSROOM ENVIRONMENT IS THE FIRST STEP IN PROVIDING A LITERATE ENVIRONMENT THAT FOSTERS READING AND WRITING TO LEARN."
>
> — Michael Conn-Powers et al.,
> "The Universal Design of Early
> Education: Moving Forward for
> All Children"

The UDL framework encourages educators to provide *multiple means of engagement*, for example, when teaching a kindergarten class about the letter *A*, the teacher can use multiple ways to engage his students by having an *A* inflatable letter, a song for *A*, letter *A* books, and video clips about *A*.

This guideline on engagement works in tandem with the next major guideline of *multiple means of representation*. Not only is the skilled teacher using different methods to engage the children, but he is also using multiple methods for teaching the letter. Children can draw the letter *A*, fingerpaint the letter, point to the letter, make the letter out of playdough, and more.

The third major guideline is of *multiple means of action and expression*. Children can demonstrate what they know in a variety of ways. The teacher can assess whether a child can recognize the letter by having him point to the letter, draw the letter, or make the letter in sand or playdough. UDL guidelines work well in a classroom that is flexible in design and supportive of various learning styles and abilities.

The principles go hand in hand with how teachers naturally create their classrooms. UDL blends what is already working and adds layers using brain-based research to make it even better. UDL approaches enable children to show their knowledge to support their skills and strengths in many ways (Conn-Powers, Cross, Traub, and Hutter-Pishgahi, 2006). All children have access to learning and have the freedom to learn. Educators work to ensure the classroom allows children to feel acknowledged as essential learners.

As the educator removes barriers to learning, children have more choices and opportunities to learn. In the past, a child diagnosed with attention-deficit hyperactivity disorder (ADHD) typically got a wiggle seat, and a child diagnosed with autism got noise-canceling headphones. While well intended, these one-size-fits-all approaches take away from child-directed learning and choices. With UDL, all children have a menu of options and, with teacher guidance, can experience and learn what works best for them. Educators can consider many factors as they implement UDL within their classrooms to facilitate a mix of independent, small-group, and whole-class learning.

Classroom Design and Layout

As we look at classroom design and layout, there are many questions to ask in creating a space that includes all children. A clear layout helps children know what to expect in each area of the classroom. There might be a quiet area, a fine-motor area, an art area, and other centers—each area has a purpose. If the classroom has everything mixed together, children can be confused about what is expected of them. A well-designed classroom also allows children to be more independent because they know where to go when the teacher says to go to the center area or book area. They do not have to rely on the adults to show them.

- Does the classroom layout allow children to move freely and have equal access to spaces and materials as their peers? For example, when a child has problems with motor planning or being able to look at a space and make choices on how to get around the room, she will struggle if the room is not arranged with clear paths. You will notice this child as the one who is often running into things or other children in the classroom. It might look like the child is doing this on purpose, but it could be that the child lacks motor-planning skills. I had a young student last year who would not walk to circle time if someone or something was in his way. This child was unable to navigate a different route and would stand, not moving. He is a bright child, but he has a weakness in motor planning. By setting up the classroom with clear routes, I was able to help him see different ways to navigate.

- Can the children safely maneuver over the different types of floor coverings? Children who have physical issues that make walking difficult or impossible, such as a child with a slight limp or a child in a wheelchair, may struggle to cross a bumpy rug or a slippery floor. I found out how difficult different surfaces could be when my son needed leg surgery and had to use a wheelchair, walker, and eventually a cane. There were many places that were no longer safe for us to go. Even a slight bump of a rug on a floor can trip a child who struggles with walking.

- Does the furniture have a purposeful placement to enhance learning? The way the room is arranged can make it easier to teach and for children to learn. By having a set area for circle time or community circle, everyone knows where to go when the teacher wants them to come together. Arrangement also sets the stage for expectations. For example, a few chairs at a table indicate that the space is used for small-group work. A spot off to one side and set up with pillows, books, and soft lighting indicate that this is a space for quiet time.

- Are the curriculum materials, technology, and learning activities accessible to all children? What changes would increase equal access for all? Children are different sizes and heights, so if all the materials are placed on high shelves, some children will not be able to reach them without help. Having everything accessible helps all the children to be independent.

- Does the classroom have flexible seating options? Flexible seating is helpful to allow children to be comfortable and have the option for movement while they learn. We will take a closer look at the benefits of flexible seating in the classroom later in this chapter.

- Is the classroom set up with flexible learning areas to allow for multiple means of representation during instruction and learning?

- Are sensory issues kept in mind in the design of the classroom? Students can struggle with lighting, clutter, textures, smells, and noise. Children can be overwhelmed by too many sensory sensations hitting them at one time. They often lack the skills to calm themselves. Are there areas where children take a break if needed? Just like adults, children need breaks to recharge, calm down, and escape possible sensory overload so they can come back refreshed and ready to learn.

Step 2: Design a Flexible and Adaptable Learning Environment

Consider purposeful classroom design. Provide a flexible learning environment that reduces barriers and increases opportunities for creating, supporting, and collaborating; provides areas for small groups and whole groups; and offers places for working independently. "Since different room arrangements serve different purposes, it is necessary for classrooms to have some degree of flexibility" (Higgins et al., 2005). In setting up the classroom environment, include the following:

- Flexible seating options

- Visual aids

- Quiet and safe learning areas

- Sensory considerations and sensory areas

- Innovative learning spaces

Flexible Learning and Seating Options

Purposeful choices for flexible seating enhance learning. "Flexible learning environments are becoming a priority in schools because they enable teachers to create unique environments that emphasize student choice" (Planbook, 2022). All children benefit from flexible learning environments that consider choice, health, comfort, community, collaboration, communication, commitment to learning, sensory input, and increased focus. "I found that as a classroom teacher, allowing students to choose the spots they found most comfortable to work in helps students concentrate and allows me to concentrate on facilitating learning, not managing behavior" (Education Technology Solutions, 2018).

- **Choice:** Children who have choices have fewer challenging behaviors because they feel like they have some control, and they also find it more fun. Choices for seating allow children to find a way that they are comfortable and can learn best. Some children like to be on a wiggle seat or an exercise ball while engaging in learning. Others would rather sit on a typical chair. The key is flexibility. Choices come with the same classroom expectations for using any materials in the classroom: If the wiggle seat goes flying through the classroom, the child loses the choice to use it until they can do so responsibly.

- **Physical health:** Children benefit from having lots of opportunities for movement, which helps to engage their brains in learning. Children who have physical limitations benefit because opportunities for movement and being near their peers help them feel more a part of the classroom community.

- **Comfort:** This is important and often overlooked. If a child is uncomfortable, they will be focusing on that instead of on learning. Think of the last time you sat in a meeting on an uncomfortable chair and how that affected your ability to focus. Children are the same way.

- **Community:** Flexible seating and classroom arrangements can make having a classroom community easier to accomplish. Providing locations for small groups and for whole groups within the classroom are a great way to build classroom community.

- **Collaboration:** A classroom layout can make it easier for students to collaborate with each other as they learn. Even the youngest child will engage and collaborate with peers when given a chance in a classroom that is set up to make this possible.

- **Communication:** Classrooms that encourage understanding and use of written and spoken language through visuals, songs, labels, and peer interactions have the flexibility to help increase children's communication skills.

- **Commitment to learning:** How the classroom is arranged affects learning. Children who can be near each other in groups have more opportunities for collaborative learning.

- **Sensory input:** The different types of seating can offer a child sensory input to help with focus and attention.

- **Increased focus:** Increased focus happens when a child is comfortable and feels safe (Planbook, 2022).

SEATING OPTIONS

Wiggle seats: Wiggle seats are wedge or round seats filled with air that allow students to wiggle while they work. These have been favorites of my students over the years.

Seats that rock: Rocking is very calming, so allowing children to rock while they sit will help them to be more relaxed and more open to learning.

Soft, round, flat seats: These seats are similar to wiggle seats, but they contain a filler instead of air to make them soft to sit on in class.

Stools: These come in assorted colors and are nice because they take up less space, allowing a table to be set up in a small area.

Exercise or balance balls: Sitting on a ball allows students to have movement and sensory input while working. I have personally seen a huge improvement in the focus of children given this option. They can bounce, rock, and move without getting out of their seats.

Regular chairs: Some children prefer a typical classroom chair without any movement or anything extra.

Crates with seats: This is another option that children find fun to sit on. They are inexpensive to make; just use a plastic crate and add a soft seat on top.

Sitting on the floor with lap trays, lap desks, or clipboards: This option allows children to move away from being at a table, desk, or traditional seating. It gives them a sturdy way to write or work on projects while using nontraditional seating.

Rugs: Rugs are softer than the hard floor and can make it easier to know that the area has a specific purpose such as circle time or community circle.

Visual Aids

Research has found that using visual aids during instruction can improve student engagement in the classroom environment. For example, one study considered many distinct categories of visual aids and found them to increase and reinforce learning and motivation (Shabiralyani et al., 2015). Instructional visuals can support learning by helping children to connect and process information. Visuals can be pictures, multimedia, objects, posters, charts, and any number of different visual ways that help children to learn. If displayed in the class, visuals can be a reference for students as they are first learning and processing new information.

Visuals can also help clarify vocabulary and concepts. For nonreaders, a visual daily schedule offers a way to organize their day so they know what is next. Place visuals in any area of the classroom where children might be expected to follow a sequence of steps, to help them learn and remember what to do. Place visual strips by center activities, such as visuals of different structures in the block area, to help children know what they can do with the materials. In addition, visuals can be used to document what children have learned. Displays of pictures of the children engaged in learning, along with documentation on the topic that they studied, let them revisit what they have learned throughout the school year.

The visuals can be objects, digital, multimedia, or on paper and composed of words, pictures, and symbols. Multimedia is a great way to take children on a virtual field trip or introduce a new unit. For example, if the teacher is talking about zoos for letter Z, visuals and multimedia are a great way to help students to better understand the concept. Visuals engage children in learning, build vocabulary, and help them make connections to prior learning to new concepts.

- **Visual schedules:** When a teacher posts a visual schedule of the day, children know what is coming next, which helps to reduce their stress and assists with independence. Visual schedules can be individualized with images attached using Velcro. A child can remove each picture as that activity is completed and know which area to move to next.

- **Visual behavior charts:** Teachers can use visuals as behavior prompts and charts to help children regulate their behavior through positive feedback. (Behavior charts should not be used to shame children or as a punishment.) Children like token charts so that they can visually see the goal they are working toward. For example, a child who likes to draw or look at books could pick a picture of that activity and then attach it to their chart, which will motivate the child to self-regulate her behavior. This approach is not just useful for a child with behavior issues; it is a great way to motivate any child. Other types of visual charts can include a small visual version of the child's daily schedule with a place for happy faces or stickers on areas that went well.

- **Visuals to adapt books and songs:** Another great way to use visuals is to adapt books. You can add visuals to any children's book to help children to better understand the story. Even books that have many visuals benefit from added images. Visuals used while singing songs help children remember the sequence of the song and allow the song to be more interactive. For example, holding up cards with numerals and images of frogs while singing "Five Little Speckled Frogs" helps children develop numeracy skills. It is also helpful to use visuals of songs during circle time, so children know what songs they are going to sing and in what order.

- **Vocabulary words and visuals:** Vocabulary words paired with visuals help students to better understand the words and make connections to support comprehension. I often search online for images to show my students when I read to them or when they read to me, if there are words that might be unfamiliar to them. They are so used to this that they will sometimes ask for pictures.

  Visual aids can also help students visualize what they have not seen before. This is important because, depending on where you are teaching, the children may have had limited experience with or not understand the topic being taught. Pictures and video clips allow children to take a virtual trip and better understand the topic. For example, I recently taught a rain forest unit. I used the smartboard and Google Earth to take them to the Amazon Rain Forest, allowing them to see all the trees and streams and really feel like they were there. I shared pictures of different animals from the rain forest, which gave the children the background knowledge they needed to start the new unit.

- **Visuals to help bridge gaps:** Visuals can bridge the gap for children struggling with auditory learning or with printed words. If a child struggles with auditory processing or has hearing problems, visuals can allow her to follow along with what her classmates are learning. Children who have frequent ear infections can have intermittent hearing loss that is not detected because it is not an issue every day. Visuals can help support them during times when they have ear infections.

- **Visual anchor charts:** Anchor charts help to show concepts and work as visual reminders in the classroom during independent work time. For example, the teacher could have a number chart with numbers and corresponding sets displayed. They could have an alphabet chart with pictures of objects that start with the sounds the letters represent. An anchor chart can be simple or complex and is helpful for any age group.

Quiet and Safe Learning Areas

In a busy classroom, a quiet and safe learning area gives children a place to focus or recharge. This space can be an area with soft furniture or mats, pillows, or beanbag chairs. The area could have books or other quiet learning items. This area should be easily visible to the teacher, so children are constantly monitored for safety. Because UDL classroom design allows for options and choices, it may be helpful to have more than one location set up. These spaces are often popular, especially for students who like quiet spots or are easily distracted.

A note of caution for quiet areas: they need to be a safe spot for any child to use, so avoid using them as a time-out space. Otherwise, instead of being a peaceful retreat, no child will want to use that space. As with introducing any new classroom area, establish clear guidelines for the children. For example, they need to use the quiet area to relax and recharge, not to jump up and down and scream. Because quiet areas do not have walls, pushing and pulling could ruin the area. Weighted lap pads, if used, are for their laps, not their heads. The basic rules are similar to the rules already in place in the classroom. Each age group will need to have rules that match their maturity level. My basic rule is that using the quiet area is a privilege, so if you are making good choices, it is something that you can use. If you are making poor choices, then someone else will get a turn and you will have to leave that area. To be honest, that is the number-one rule that works well. I have had teachers tell me that the quiet area doesn't work because students are knocking everything over and no one wants to use it. When I observe, I will find out that it is being used as a time-out space, so the children do not want to use it because everyone will think they are in trouble. Instead, if you notice a child needs a break in the quiet area, offer it as a choice. By knowing your students, you start to recognize the warning signs of a meltdown or challenging behavior. That is the best time to intervene and offer a child a choice to take a break. The child will have an opportunity to calm down and not be embarrassed due to the way the teacher handled the situation.

Quiet areas can be used in a number of ways. The quiet area is one tool to help children calm down. For example, children struggle to regulate and calm down when they have big emotions or feel overwhelmed. Adults need to teach and show them ways to calm themselves. An out-of-control or upset child cannot learn new information. When children are calmer, they can relax and focus on learning. If one of your students is upset and has her head down on the desk instead of engaging in the lesson, a quick break is often enough to shift the focus away from what is bothering her and allow her to engage in learning again. Some quiet areas have headphones so children can listen to soft music. A relaxed child will return to the group feeling better, recharged, and ready to join the group again. It is a simple concept, yet very effective.

Some quiet areas can be set up as an option for independent learning. There might be books or puzzles for younger children or learning centers for older children. With fewer distractions, they can complete the task given to them. I have had students request to go to the quiet area to look at or read books because they prefer to be away from their louder peers.

Sensory Considerations and Sensory Areas

According to a 2012 article by early childhood specialist Suzanne Gainsley, sensory areas are "food for the brain." She explains that sensory experiences send signals to the brain that improve neural pathways during children's investigations and learning. As children are exploring and using the sensory area, they are making brain connections and learning through play.

The sensory area is great for all children, not just those with sensory sensitivities or behavior concerns. It is a place to calm down and recharge while investigating the different materials available. Sometimes, I will use specific items at the table for the students to sort into categories such as rough and smooth or soft and hard. I have set up a container with water and let them explore items that sink or float. When using the sensory area as a place where children can calm down, the key is to offer the choice of the sensory area when they are showing signs of distress and not wait until they are out of control. Once a child is out of control, the sensory area is no longer an option.

> Sam, age five, had frequent behavior outbursts in the classroom. He threw chairs, yelled, kicked, hit, and rarely followed directions. He was not a child on the autism spectrum, nor did he have any sensory issues. But the sensory area ended up being a place that worked for him and other students with challenging behavior. His teacher and his therapist

discussed the challenges Sam was experiencing and decided to offer sensory breaks for him during the day.

Watching him calm down while engaged in the sensory area was fascinating. This one simple change to his environment significantly affected his learning ability and behavior. He was calmer and more focused. Although he still had behavior-management issues, the sensory table was successful.

Sam's story is an excellent example of the importance of UDL principles in the environment.

Sensory stimuli are often an issue for people with autism and other disabilities. In her book *Thinking in Pictures*, Temple Grandin, a scientist and advocate for people with autism, and her coauthor Oliver Sacks (2006) explain that the brains of people who are neurodivergent, such as people with autism, are different from neurotypical people and that people with many types of variable learning issues also have difficulties with sensory integration.

Some of the problems come from the way they feel and the way their brains process sensory information. It is as if they have oversensitive sensory receptors, so any sensory stimulus is coming in full force. For example, a neurotypical child can ignore most noises in the classroom, but for a child with sensory integration issues, noises will seem loud and may even hurt their ears. They are unable to work because they are in distress. Picture yourself walking into a large dance hall with disco lights going and a band playing loudly, and you are told to quietly read a book. Your sensory system would be overloaded, which would inhibit your ability to focus. This is what is happening to children with sensory integration difficulties. They are being overwhelmed by the sensory overload and struggle to calm down enough to learn. This is why some children will wear noise-cancellation headphones. Others might prefer fewer lights or table lamps instead of overhead lights. Their parents may pick soft clothes that do not have tags or may cut out the tags, because even something as simple as a tag can keep a child from focusing. It is often hard for teachers to believe this because a child with sensory issues can be loud, and the child's own noise doesn't bother her. But keep in mind, the noise a child makes is one she has control over and can stop. This is different from noise that the child has no control over.

Sensory areas offer some key benefits.

- **Opportunity for sensory exploration:** When children are exploring in the sensory area, they are learning and making brain connections. This is why the sensory area is good for all children and is not just a special-education section of the classroom.

- **Language development and increased socialization:** Children have opportunities to increase social skills while they work together and take turns in the sensory area. They will also self-talk while they are exploring.

- **Cognitive development:** Sensory play can support cognitive development as children solve problems, make connections, and form conclusions while playing. Sensory and academic skills can be integrated when the sensory bins contain letters or numbers for students to find and sort. Using sand to trace letters and numbers is another fun sensory way to learn. Making letters, numbers, and beginning words from playdough or by painting are just a few of the many ways that the sensory area can support students' cognitive development.

- **Regulating emotions:** As already discussed, sensory areas are great for helping children calm down. A child engaged in the sensory area can relax and recharge from the busy classroom (Salus University Occupational Therapy Institute, 2021).

- **Fine-motor skills:** The sensory area is also a wonderful place for children to work on fine-motor skills without knowing they are working on these skills. They can strengthen hand muscles by using playdough. They can pour, sort, and manipulate the different supplies and materials.

Keep in mind the age and interest of the children when considering what to use for the sensory area. Ensure that all materials are nontoxic. The items in the sensory area can be changed according to the skills and abilities of the students.

If you do not have much room for a sensory area, or if you want to offer lots of options for sensory explorations, consider creating sensory tubs. Ideas include using theme bins and storybook bins filled with items related to learning objectives. You can fill containers with paper or fabric scraps, water, playdough, pompoms, balls with various textures, ice, and fidgets. You can provide a variety of textures to explore, including sandpaper, fur, cotton, plastic items, large beads, steel wool, foil, sand, pine cones, bubble wrap, and more. You can offer science explorations, such as pouring water into different-sized containers; sorting objects by size, color, or shape; child-friendly magnets to see what they can pick up; and mixing and exploring paint colors. Offer mini-experiments, such as the opportunity to see what happens to a premade mini-volcano when children add baking soda and vinegar. (My kindergarteners loved this experiment. I made mini-volcanoes from little milk cartons and clay. We reset the experiment for each group.)

Weighted Lap Pads and Stuffed Animals

Weighted items are calming for children and help with focus. They should be kept separate from the sensory area, so the teacher can monitor their use. It is essential to consult your school's occupational therapist to determine recommendations for weight and length of use. There are guidelines for every age group. I kept a container of weighted lap pads in the classroom that anyone could use at any time. The most common use was during circle time, but children also like to have them when they worked at the tables or desks. I have found that all the children like using weighted items.

You can add extra weight to stuffed animals by opening a seam, adding weighted beads, then stitching the seam closed again. Each child can hold one in circle time; I find the children get up less and are more focused when they have something on their lap that has a little weight. Like any item in the classroom, children must follow the classroom rules and make good choices to use a weighted item. My rules are that children cannot put the weighted items on their heads, throw them, or sit on them. (The no-sitting rule came after a child had a potty accident on one of the lap pads.)

Step 3: Create a Clutter-Free, Well-Organized Classroom

Entering some classrooms can cause an immediate overload. When teachers display multiple learning posters and offer unorganized materials scattered throughout the room, children who have difficulty processing visual information, and even typical learners, can be overwhelmed and unable to find the information they need for learning. Any clutter is stressful and distracts from learning.

Set up a stimulating and enriching environment that includes hands-on materials children can explore, ask questions about, and experiment with while learning. Such an environment promotes language through songs, rhymes, books, centers, and movement as children develop stronger language and communication skills. It should be an environment that encourages exploration and provides materials and access to learning that is age appropriate and moves with the pace of young children.

When designing a classroom with UDL, it is helpful to think of minimalism. Everything should serve a purpose. Materials, equipment, and furniture contribute to the overall environment and learning philosophy. Many teachers are already naturally incorporating some UDL principles in their classroom environment; other educators require assistance from their organized friends. The best way to set up a UDL classroom is to consider the classroom's goals and objectives and make sure it contains everything that the children need to learn accessible for them. Consider who will be using the classroom and the ages and abilities of the students.

Another way to organize an early childhood classroom is by creating natural boundaries. These areas could be set up with the quiet area, center area, circle time area, table area, art, and sensory area (Tracy, 2019). For example, use yellow tape on the floor to show where center items need to stay or where to line up. You can create boundaries with furniture, putting bookshelves or center shelves strategically around the classroom to give each area its own space. Once you have created the boundaries, teach the students the expectations for each area. The classroom should be adapted and safe for the age that is using the classroom.

Have enough space so that there is room for whole-group and small-group lessons. Provide a variety of learning areas to help maintain the children's interest and allow for exploration and engaging learning throughout their day. The space should be arranged so that the different areas of the classroom are easy to find and well defined. Students should have easy access and should know what materials they can access independently and which areas need teacher permission. The spaces should include indoor and outdoor spaces if possible, so students can have plenty of movement activities. Everything should be set up so the teacher can always see all the children for safety (Quebec Education Program, Preschool Education, 2021).

Step 4: Develop a Positive Classroom-Management Plan

All behavior is communication. The challenge for the teacher is to be a detective and work toward figuring out what message a behavior is communicating. One strategy for evaluating child behavior involves identifying the ABCs of the behavior:

- **A is for *antecedent*:** The events or actions before a behavior can offer clues about why and with whom the behavior is happening.

- **B for is *behavior*:** What exactly is the child doing?

- **C for is *consequences*:** What happens immediately after the behavior?

By charting this information, teachers can look for patterns in the child's behavior to determine what the child is trying to communicate. For example, sometimes students consistently fall apart during a specific subject, following a change in schedule, due to sensory overload, or when they are coming down with a cold or flu. Maybe the child is afraid of another student outside who sometimes bullies them, and the teacher will need to address the bullying. Perhaps the child has sensory issues, so she falls apart whenever the school has an event where multiple classes are together. A child may be seeking the teacher's attention, even when it is negative; she can learn to earn one-on-one time with the teacher by making better choices. For other children, struggles on a particular day of the week could result from a different schedule that day. Teachers have to be detectives to look at the behavior data and determine the cause and what the student needs and is trying to communicate.

This information tells the teacher where to put additional scaffolding to support the child. For example, if a child falls apart for schedule changes, she may benefit from a visual schedule or simply being told that a change is about to happen, depending on her needs. This way, the child will know of changes in advance.

Offer Choices and Flexibility

Classroom management plans that incorporate choices, flexibility, and the range of classroom needs work best. Offering the children choices and stimulating instruction increases their engagement and learning and decreases challenging behavior. Flexibility and meeting the needs of the children will also dramatically reduce behavior challenges in the classroom.

Often students with behavior issues face significant barriers that are so great that they give up. They may try to hide their insecurities by acting out. For example, a child with academic challenges or who struggles with staying focused might not want her peers to know she cannot keep up. That child might prefer to get in trouble for behavior than be embarrassed by making a mistake. Knowing a child's learning profile, interventions, methods used, and UDL guidelines can help you meet the child's needs and reduce their impulse to act out.

For example, I once worked with a bright student who struggled with focus and impulsivity, so he performed far below his abilities in math class. He was embarrassed by his poor math grades and his struggles to answer his teacher's questions correctly. Instead of writing down the wrong answers, he would rip up his paper or refuse to work. Other times, he acted like the class clown, significantly disrupting the class. His most significant barrier was his poor focus, so he missed important information that his teacher and classmates shared. This lack of focus cause him to perform poorly in his work, which led him to engage in disruptive behavior. It became a cycle that he couldn't break on his own. He needed interventions to have success.

Clearly Communicate Expectations

Design and support a positive classroom and school culture to proactively maximize learning with clear routines and expectations. Build and foster relationships with students; children need to trust before they can learn. Greet them as they arrive in your classroom. Get on their level and get involved in projects and play. Make them feel that what they say and do is valued and important by really listening to them when they speak. Community circles and classroom group activities can also help build teacher-student relationships and a positive classroom that learns to work together.

Classroom reward systems are a way to promote a positive classroom, but keep in mind the needs of your students. For example, if some children need help to meet a specific goal, a whole-class group reward may not be suitable. However, this method can work well for classes in which all the students can successfully work toward a goal. Avoid creating a reward system in which one child or a few children might cause the class to miss out on a prize, thus upsetting their peers and putting these children at risk of being bullied. Before using this method, know your students and what they can do together.

Clear expectations and routines make it easier for children to navigate their day and be more independent. For example, a teacher might place colored dots on the floor in a line, so when it is time to line up and change activities or leave the classroom, children can independently walk to the line and stand on a dot. This way, students are spaced evenly, ready to go. Some teachers assign a particular dot color to each student, so the children know which dot is for them. Other teachers use a number system, and students old enough to remember a number can quickly get in the correct order. The strategies you choose will depend on the students' age and abilities. Experiment and see which system works best for the children you work with. That said, avoid changing strategies too quickly; if a teacher has children line up by the tables one day and by the whiteboard the next day, the students will likely react with more behavior challenges and need more teacher guidance to find their place. The same goes for expectations. If one student is allowed to jump around the class without a consequence but another gets in trouble for the same behavior, the mixed messages and inconsistency cause confusion and more behavioral incidents.

Transitions among classroom options and activities can be challenging. One effective method is for the teacher to have a cueing system for transitions or to gain children's attention. Songs, visuals, doorbells, and chimes can be successful. A teacher at my school uses a classroom doorbell system for transitions, which works great. The sound is pleasant and comes with a button for the teacher and a device that plugs into an outlet. The children know to stop and listen for instructions whenever they hear the sound.

For students old enough to care for their personal needs independently, they might use a hand signal to alert their teacher that they need a bathroom break, so the class can continue working. The teacher can convey nonverbally that this is okay.

Teachers can cue children in other ways. For example, some wear visuals on their lanyards that indicate expectations for students, such as a picture of a student sitting, a picture of a quiet voice, or any classroom expectation. Children respond well to visuals, which can remind a particular child without drawing attention from the rest of the class. Classroom visuals to remind children of expectations can help all students be successful. For example, there could be a partner or whisper sign for when the class uses partner work and a classroom sign for quiet talking when working together in groups. The visual cues help children understand that the voice-level expectations change throughout the school day depending on the classroom activity.

Positive incentives work well to promote a positive classroom atmosphere. The rewards can be as simple as being allowed to go without their shoes while in the classroom or bringing a favorite stuffed animal to school.

Incorporate the UDL guidelines into the classroom positive management plan through engagement, representation, action, and expression. The goal is to create a healthy, positive, comfortable, safe, and secure atmosphere to support students in a stimulating and enriching environment by using knowledge of the students and their needs.

Build a Positive School-Wide Culture

Although educators have limited control over the whole school culture, they can advocate for and help build it. As children go to specials, lunch, and other areas of the building, those areas need to be safe, supportive, and part of the school-wide positive behavior plan. Each team member is an integral part of the children's journey and can make a difference in a child's ability to thrive and grow in academics and social-emotional development. The following is an example of the need to include all children in a positive school-wide culture.

> I taught seven- to nine-year-old children with significant cognitive disabilities in a self-contained classroom for seven years. The school was a school of the arts, which one year put on a school-wide dance routine with music that the children had learned in their music classes.

Watching the outdoor performance was fantastic. But then one of my students said our class did not get to participate because they were in the "dumb" class. No one thought about including my students.

When we returned to the classroom, he took out his frustration by destroying his pencil box of supplies and was unhappy the rest of the day. You can imagine his academic ability had been significantly affected by being left out and not treated equally. He carried this feeling over into the next few days and exhibited many behaviors that could have been avoided had these students been included.

Step 5: It Is Okay to Start Small and Not Try to Do It All

Like UDL for students, teachers have choices too. Target an area of UDL and begin one step at a time. Even small changes will help students to be more successful. Set obtainable goals, implement UDL one step at a time, and build a more inclusive and equitable classroom for all students.

• • •

The classroom environment significantly affects children and their learning. UDL works well in a classroom that is flexible in design and supportive of various learning styles and abilities. When setting up the classroom to be engaging and equitable, more children are able to access what they need to succeed. The flexible, adaptable learning environment using the UDL mindset allows for multiple means of representation, multiple means of action and expression, and multiple means of engagement. Using the minimalist methods will create a clutter-free, well-organized classroom where children can locate key learning areas and freely move about in the classroom. The positive classroom management plan is a way to help students to feel safe, know their boundaries, and build a positive classroom community. Rethinking and redesigning the classroom will create an environment that is safe, equitable, and accessible, and that permits all students to thrive.

CHAPTER 4
Learner Variability and UDL

"Learner variability should be seen, understood, and honored as a personal asset."
• **Kathleen McClaskey (2022)** •

Learner variability is the distinct group of skills and experiences that each child has when it comes to learning (Vuchic and Pape, 2018). Each child has a learner profile with their own learning variabilities. For example, a child could be talented in math but need extra help in reading. Another could have sensory issues, and another child might come from a difficult environment. Universal design for learning can empower children by giving them tools to help them thrive with their unique set of skills. This chapter describes some of the many different types of learner variabilities, but it isn't an exhaustive list. This chapter is not meant to be a diagnostic tool or a reason to exclude children but to give examples of the many ways learning can be affected and to share some possible accommodations to help each child to be successful.

Educators often have little training regarding learning variabilities, making planning for the children's varying needs challenging. The information in this chapter is a starting point of ideas for incorporating changes that can help children to be successful in the classroom. When planning, consider having accommodations easily accessible to all learners. Children vary by what they need, even throughout their day, and learn best when guided by the teacher as they make decisions and choices on what helps them become expert learners. Options give students more control of their learning and help them develop lifelong skills to make decisions while learning (Pape, 2018).

Children do not need a label, an IEP, or a 504 plan to receive an accommodation that would help them succeed. Accommodations are tools that can break down barriers to learning. Ideally, assistive technology should be as easy to access as a pencil and paper. This chapter does describe several learning variabilities; if you notice characteristics that fall into particular categories, then the accommodations listed might be helpful for any child who has similar characteristics.

Behavioral Learning Variabilities

Children may not have the label of ADHD or ASD, but the teacher may notice that some struggle with many of the common characteristics of these challenges. Using strategies described in each category will help children's learning as well as classroom management. As mentioned, a label is not necessary for interventions to start. Early interventions are the key to success.

Attention Deficit Hyperactivity Disorder (ADHD)

According to the Centers for Disease Control and Prevention (CDC, 2022c), there are three types of ADHD:

- **Predominantly Inattentive Presentation:** child struggles to focus and attend to key details in instructions or conversations

- **Predominantly Hyperactive-Impulsive Presentation:** child is constantly in motion, running, jumping, fidgeting, and climbing, and may blurt out and interrupt

- **Combined Presentation:** child has a combination of both types

Children with ADHD often play with anything they can find. Erasers become racecars. Pencils are airplanes. They are aware of every noise and every person walking by. They struggle to focus on what is essential. They have a hard time filtering out extraneous noises and activities around them. On the other hand, if they are highly interested in something, they can hyper-focus.

Some common characteristics in children with ADHD are blurting out during class, daydreaming, having deficits in cognitive functioning, difficulty staying focused, being easily distracted, hyperactivity, impulsiveness, and inattentiveness (Gawrilow et al., 2013).

Accommodations and modifications can help a child be successful in a classroom setting. Movement is essential for all children and is especially helpful for those with ADHD. Educators can get children active in many creative ways that allow for action and movement during the school day, including brain breaks, hands-on projects, and placing learning activities in several spots or centers around the classroom. A child could deliver an envelope to a teacher who knows the plan. One creative art teacher worked out a plan with a child's classroom teacher to allow the child to bring her a golden paintbrush. She would give the child a five-minute project, such as working with clay or painting a picture, and then send the child back to the classroom refreshed and ready to work again. Collaborate with other team members on ways to encourage positive behavior interventions and movement throughout the children's day.

Preferential seating—placing a child in the best location to thrive in your classroom—is mentioned often in the accommodation list for learning variabilities. Seating could be near the teacher, in a quiet spot away from distractions, in a location where a child can move more easily, or near a peer helper. One year I had a child who was selectively mute, so I placed her next to her friends to encourage talking. Children who are active might have options of standing or using different types of seating while engaged in activities.

Movement should also include daily outside time when the weather permits. According to a study of 421 children, outdoor play in green spaces significantly reduced the severity of ADHD symptoms. This is important for educators, because play is often not considered an important part of a child's day at school (Faber Taylor and Kuo, 2011).

Autism Spectrum Disorder (ASD)

ASD is a neurological syndrome that can affect a child's communication, learning, and behavior (National Institute of Mental Health, 2022). Common characteristics can include anxiety; auditory-processing issues; delayed social skills; difficulty recognizing personal space; difficulty understanding nonverbal communication; difficulty with multistep directions; literal thinking; lack of eye contact; obsession with a specific topic or item; poor problem-solving skills; problems with eating due to sensory sensitivities that might limit a child's diet; issues sleeping, which can affect the child's school day when they arrive tired; sensory sensitivities; speech and language delays or difficulty understanding pragmatic language; struggles with changes and with regulating their emotions, and uneven skills. Children with ASD are frequent targets of teasing and bullying.

At one time, ASD and Asperger's syndrome were considered different disorders. Currently, autism and Asperger's are included under the umbrella of autism spectrum disorder. This can be confusing for teachers because children will vary in the characteristics they exhibit. Autism can range from a child with an intellectual disability who is nonverbal to a brilliant child who exhibits quirky sensory sensitivities and social struggles. As researcher Christopher Frauenberger cautions, "If you have seen one child with autism, you have seen one child with autism" (Frauenberger, 2015).

One in 44 children has ASD (CDC, 2022a, 2022c). In his book *The Complete Guide to Asperger's Syndrome,* Tony Attwood (2015) explains that it is like they are on a train, and if something gets in their way, they become stuck. In contrast, he compares the general population to people who are riding in all-terrain vehicles and can problem-solve ways to get around the obstacle. In people with ASD, inflexible and literal thinking are frequent causes of meltdowns. They need help to look at other possibilities. For example, if a child wants to be the first in line but must wait for another day, this might cause a meltdown because he sees only one way and that is to be first. He struggles to problem solve that it will be okay to wait until tomorrow.

Children with ASD can be literal thinkers; do not assume students are on the same page with you. For example, if someone tells them to work independently, they will not ask for help if they get stuck because they take "work independently" literally and will not accept help. Lack of understanding and literal thinking can cause unnecessary confusion or meltdowns. Once, I told Eli (the child in the story on page 5) that he needed to wear his coat outside. He was refusing to do so. I said in jest, "Your dad would shoot me if I let you go out in the cold without your coat." Eli looked thoughtfully at me and said, "My dad would never shoot you; he cares about you and would only help you." I had to explain that I was kidding.

LIFE WITH A CHILD WHO HAS AUTISM

When families have children with learning variabilities, it is essential to understand that some have been through many traumatic and frightening experiences. Have an open heart when working with them as you collaborate to help their child to reach their full potential.

When Brett was three years old, his parents took the family to church one Sunday. Brett didn't like the noise and took off, covering his ears, and hid under a church pew. The family finally had to leave because he was disruptive and unhappy. Later, Brett's mom took him and his sisters to the grocery store. Before they could finish loading their cart and check out, Brett had one of his meltdowns, so they left the cart at the store and went home without groceries.

The parents fought about who would bathe Brett because giving him a bath was like bathing a puppy. Brett was also still getting up every night and needed little sleep. His family was under constant stress. His sisters, who were in elementary school, missed having time to read books or do their homework with parental support because of the attention Brett needed.

One weekend, a family get-together was cut short because everyone blamed Brett's parents for his behavior. Later in the week, a trip to the library also ended early when Brett started pulling books off a shelf. His mother saw other families enjoying story time while she left with Brett and his sisters. The girls cried because they did not get to check out books, and Brett was upset about leaving too. In an attempt to salvage some of the day, Brett's mom stopped and got them ice cream cones. The girls were excited, but Brett cried because his ice cream cone was too cold and he wanted to put it in the microwave to warm it up. He sobbed on the way home.

Characteristics of ASD can affect a child's learning and peer relationships. For example, a child who doesn't understand personal space often touches or runs into peers. In this case, the teacher must work with the child on a plan to help him succeed. The teacher may use a chart on which the child earns stickers for keeping his hands to himself. Or, the teacher may give the child a fidget to provide little hands with something appropriate to do.

A child with ASD can have uneven skills, appearing to be advanced in some areas yet having significant delays in other areas of development. Inconsistent skills can confuse educators who wonder how a young child can recite all their letters and numbers but cannot apply that knowledge. For example, several years ago, I had a five-year-old student with ASD who could recognize any instrument he heard in a song. It was an amazing gift, but he also ate nonedible items. Any teacher might expect a child with brilliant skills would also know they cannot eat crayons and dirt. Still, the brain is a mystery, and how it is wired can vary, causing a mixture of skills.

In the early childhood classroom, it helps to break down steps to avoid overwhelming a child. For example, if the children are doing projects, a child with ASD or with focus issues would do best with only a few steps at a time. If the activity involves anything messy, the child may need alternate ways to work while keeping her hands clean. Directions should be clear and concise or conveyed nonverbally with visuals. Build independent skills by adding visual strips with picture steps for frequently used activities that have multiple steps.

Have a good classroom-management plan with clear expectations, and model what is expected. Children with focus issues or ASD struggle with disorganization and changes in the schedule.

Consistent schedules and routines can help children understand what is coming next and what is expected. For example, they may have visuals to help them remember to stay in their area by sitting or standing, to use kind words, and to keep their hands to themselves.

Some helpful assistive technology includes noise-canceling headphones, which are beneficial for children who are bothered by noise or are easily distracted. They can play with fidgets to help them focus and be calmer while working or playing. Weighted lap pads or stuffed animals are calming and help children stay seated in their chairs or during circle time. Wiggle seats, exercise balls, or different types of flexible seating are helpful for the child with ASD. Flexible seating allows children to move and helps with sensory input and comfort during learning or relaxing. Allowing children to stand while working is an excellent strategy for children who crave movement. Preferential seating within the classroom will allow the child to be placed in a location with room for movement and away from possible distractions. Sometimes, a child may need a separate space near their peers as they learn impulse control.

Another strategy is to give children a break in the sensory or quiet classroom area. The quiet area could be a study carrel or a DIY study area (see directions on page 117). After a break, children are calmer and recharged, enabling them to return to the group to learn.

Social stories can be beneficial for all children, including those with ADHD or ASD. They involve writing about or dictating to a teacher what they did and how their actions affected others, followed by what they can do next. Together, the teacher and child add visuals and text that the teacher reads or the student reads with the teacher. These stories help children to see how their actions affect others and understand ideas for making better choices in the future. For example, one year I had a five-year-old student with ASD who was screaming and throwing wood chips at his friend at recess. Using a social story helped him understand his actions and how the other child felt. After hearing the social story about how his friend felt sad when he screamed and threw wood chips, he cried. He had no idea that his method of getting the other person's attention was inappropriate. I worked with him to replace the unwanted behavior with waving and saying hi when he saw his friend at recess. This worked well and stopped the unwanted behavior.

Speech, Hearing, and Auditory Processing

Speech and Language Challenges

Sometimes, children experience a delay in their language development. This could be in their *pragmatic language*, which is knowing how to take turns when communicating, listening, voice control, staying on topic, and personal space. A delay may show up in *receptive language*, which is the ability to understand what they hear, or in *expressive language*, which is the ability to communicate. Sometimes, children struggle with articulation and need to work on sound production so they can speak more clearly. It is always good to have a hearing test to rule out hearing issues. Some children with frequent ear infections have intermittent hearing loss due to fluid in their ears, which can cause speech and language delays.

Auditory Processing Disorder

Auditory processing disorder is when a child can hear but has poor processing skills, difficulty blocking out noise in the classroom, and difficulty focusing on what is essential. The child may seem deaf, yet can pass a basic hearing test. The problem occurs because the brain struggles to process the auditory information it receives (Griffiths, 2002).

Common characteristics of auditory processing disorder include difficulty distinguishing sounds correctly, tracking sounds, filtering out background noise, and challenges with listening skills. For example, when a teacher talks, the typical child can focus on what the teacher is saying. Still, a child with auditory processing disorder may also hear the fan in the classroom, other children moving in their seats, and noises outside the classroom. It is as if the child has an antenna that picks up every noise, and the child's brain cannot focus on what is essential, which confuses her. This is why visuals are so important. The child can see and hear to help with processing while learning. Visuals for children with auditory processing are like glasses for children with vision issues. They allow children to learn with their visual strength without being limited by their poor auditory processing skills.

Hearing Impairment

Hearing impairment means that a child has mild to moderate hearing loss, which can be permanent or may be temporary due to wax or fluid buildup in their ears. A child does not have to be deaf for hearing loss to significantly affect academic and language development. Sometimes, a child cannot hear specific frequencies, making speech exceedingly difficult to understand.

Common characteristics of hearing impairment include difficulty in hearing when there is background noise and the resulting social effects from an inability to communicate effectively. Children with hearing impairment may exhibit some characteristics of a child with ADHD because they cannot hear well. For example, they may quickly become distracted and off task. If a teacher is concerned about a child, she should not try to diagnose a condition, but rather bring any concerns to the school nurse and the child's family, mentioning only what she has observed. The family may then want to ask their child's doctor for advice. Hearing tests at school can find some types of losses. Still, they are less high-tech than having a professional audiologist and an ear, nose, and throat specialist examine the child. Early interventions can mean the difference between a child ending up with a lifelong disability or receiving the necessary interventions.

Accommodations and Modifications for Speech, Hearing, and Auditory Processing Issues

COMMUNICATION BOOK

If a child has a communication delay, it is essential to find ways to help her communicate her needs and wants. One way is to create a communication book with frequently used pictures paired with words. I put an example and directions for a DIY communication book on page 128. I teach children to use the book by starting with a preferred toy or food picture and rewarding them for asking and showing the picture. Then, I can keep adding images to give them more communication opportunities. Frequently used picture cards might include *bathroom*, *drink*, different school activities, and anything critical for the child, depending on her age. I also put a Velcro sentence starter on the front of the book. Sentence starters can include "I want," "I need," and "I like" to increase communication skills. A child can pull the correct sentence starter and then add an image. For example, the child may put "I want" along with a picture of pretzels. The teacher can then encourage the child to say, "I want pretzels," while sharing the sentence strip. The idea is to build language skills and encourage the child to speak beyond saying single words or not talking at all.

ASSISTIVE TECHNOLOGY

Other accommodations for language and auditory development include the use of assistive technology. Some assistive technology—called augmentative and alternative communication (AAC)—includes communication books, tablets with pictures or words, or any device with pictures or words that allows a child to communicate. Assistive listening devices and FM devices can help a child who struggles to focus on a teacher's voice among all the other classroom sounds. Assistive listening devices are worn by both the child and teacher and allow the child to receive the teacher's voice directly to their ears. FM devices broadcast signals through a radio system, putting the teacher's voice above the other noise in the classroom, and can help all children focus better on the teacher's voice. The teacher wears a microphone that hooks into the system in the classroom. The mic can also be passed to students to use when speaking (McPherson, 2022).

Two computer programs that help with auditory processing and language skills include Earobics and Fast ForWord (Campbell, 2011). Earobics is designed for children ages four to seven and is an option for home or school settings. Fast ForWord is a high-tech, more expensive, and more intensive program for ages five and up. Both programs have interactive games that ask the child to click on matching sounds or find a sequence of pictures. They have mixed results, with some children making more progress than others. I mention these programs because the results can be remarkable for the right child. An educator can write a grant request for the funds to purchase these programs; they must be used by a speech pathologist or someone who has been trained on how to use the programs and the data they create. The teacher can use these programs at a learning center or with small groups to work on auditory processing and listening skills, as well as beginning reading skills. They also work well for children who are English language learners.

We used both programs with our son when he was four to seven years old. They were among many tools we found beneficial in developing his language and auditory processing skills. Other assistive technology includes captioned media, which is excellent with songs or video clips used in the classroom. Children have fun and increase their language and reading skills using captioned media.

OTHER COMMUNICATION OPTIONS

Visuals are critical for children with hearing, auditory, and language issues because they are such a powerful tool for learning. Additional ways to encourage language are through music, books, and rhymes. Sign language can also be helpful as children learn to communicate. Before my son started talking, he learned beginning sign language. His first word was *more* to ask for more juice. Sign language opened the door to additional communication.

Minimizing distractions and background noise is essential for children with hearing and auditory issues. The more noise in the background, the less they can hear or understand. Preferential seating to place a child near instruction and away from distractions can be helpful, as can providing a quiet space, such as a study carrel or DIY study area, where the child can concentrate. The quiet area is especially beneficial for children who need to focus on completing projects or assignments.

Other accommodations include ensuring children can see the teacher's face and that the teacher can get a child's attention before speaking. Teachers should check for understanding and use clear, concise directions. Because of the extra strain of trying to follow the teacher and peers when they communicate together, children with auditory challenges benefit from occasional breaks (Crouse, 2019). It is also helpful to raise awareness in the class of hearing-related concerns through age-appropriate books.

Early childhood teachers are key for intervening and providing children with the support they need to be successful later in life. A speech teacher is a good resource for additional ways to support language development in the classroom. These professionals have specialized training and access to helpful resources for teachers and families.

Vision Impairment

Vision impairment is a condition in which a child has mild to moderate vision loss. It can be caused by various eye, optic nerve, and brain disorders. For example, a child could struggle with weak eye muscles that cause the eyes to turn in or out or cause problems with eye-tracking (Dale, Salt, Sargent, and Greenaway, 2022).

Accommodations for Vision Challenges

Some possible accommodations include high-contrast learning materials and large print materials that are easier to see. Hands-on learning materials, manipulatives, raised-line paper, and tactile models can help a child with visual challenges understand what is being taught. For example, wooden or plastic shapes can help with understanding the characteristics of different shapes. Plastic letters and numbers can help a child understand the features of letters and numbers.

The best resource is the child's family and the knowledge shared by their eye doctor. Depending on the severity of the visual issue, the educator may need to consult with the district vision specialist. The American Foundation for the Blind also offers many resources for teachers and families.

Some eye problems can be prevented if a child has treatment before age eight. Regular eye checkups are essential for all children. A pediatrician can check for minor eye issues but cannot test for more significant eye problems. An ophthalmologist can do more extensive tests, even on the eyes of babies. My daughter cooperated for the pediatrician—sort of. She insisted on testing only one eye, but we assumed she was a typical four-year-old being fussy. I had gotten glasses as a baby, so we watched her for eye problems. We found out later at the eye doctor that our daughter's vision loss in her other eye was so severe that she was legally blind in that eye. If we had waited a couple more years, she would have lost all vision in that eye. Yet, undergoing surgery and wearing patches and glasses as a young child helped ensure her vision.

Learning Disabilities in K–3

This section focuses on children in kindergarten through third grade. In children ages three and four, some developmental issues might seem age appropriate, but as children develop and the gap between peers widens, different types of learning disabilities can show up. This doesn't mean that three- and four-year-olds could not have some learning disabilities listed. It is just harder to know at that age if they are struggling due to a learning disability, are a late bloomer, or have medical issues that could interfere with learning. For example, three- and four-year-olds are beginning to learn letters and sounds. By kindergarten, they should be able to connect many letters with the sounds they represent. If a child is well below her peers, and a medical issue has been ruled out as a factor, the child could have a learning disability that is interfering with her learning and development. Another example is writing. Three- and four-year-olds often scribble or write large and hard-to-read letters and numbers mixed with other marks. As children develop, the expected norm changes. What is considered okay at age three could be considered evidence of a disability at age seven.

The National Association of Special Education Teachers (2022) uses *neurological disorders* as an umbrella term that refers to issues affecting spoken language, reading (dyslexia), math (dyscalculia), and written language (dysgraphia). These disorders affect the brain's ability to receive, process, and respond, causing a child to perform below the expected level for their age.

There are many types of learning disabilities, the characteristics of which depend on the type and severity of the disability. Let's look at some of the most common in the kindergarten-to-third-grade range.

Dyslexia and Reading Disabilities

According to the International Dyslexia Association, *dyslexia* is a neurobiological learning disability in which the affected person has difficulties with decoding, reading fluency, comprehension, and phonetic skills. Dyslexia may cause a delay in the development of vocabulary and background knowledge. People with dyslexia often exhibit poor processing, tracking, and spelling skills. They may lack stamina due to the amount of effort that it takes to read. Dyslexia is not related to cognitive abilities or inadequate instruction (International Dyslexia Association, 2022). Children usually start to be diagnosed when they are five or six years old and begin to learn phonemic awareness and reading skills. Some states require dyslexia testing to start in kindergarten. People who have the disorder are at a higher risk of dropping out of school (Nash, 2017).

In children who are dyslexic and have a family history of dyslexia, brain studies show slower development in the left hemisphere of the brain and faster growth in the right hemisphere. The research shows a correlation between brain development and reading problems in children (Ostertag et al., 2021). Fifteen to twenty percent of people in the United States exhibit symptoms of dyslexia.

The following are some effective accommodations and modifications teachers can use for children with reading disabilities.

- **Consider the lighting:** Some readers struggle with fluorescent lighting and glare. Color overlays placed over book pages can be helpful in reducing glare.

- **Provide bookmarks:** With dyslexia, eye tracking can also be a problem. Bookmarks help struggling readers keep their place.

- **Consider using digital books:** E-books can have adjustable print sizes and background colors to make reading easier.

- **Use audiobooks:** Some online book services, such as Learning Ally, Epic Books, and Tumble Books, can read books aloud to the children. When students are old enough to take tests, the test can be read aloud when reading is not being tested.

Dysgraphia and Writing Disabilities

Dysgraphia is a neurological issue that causes writing difficulties. A child might struggle with spacing, forming, and copying letters (National Institute of Neurological Disorders and Stroke, 2022). Types of dysgraphia include processing, motor, and spatial. *Processing dysgraphia* relates to how the brain processes and affects working memory; *motor dysgraphia* is due to difficulty with fine-motor skills and the ability to have a proper pencil grip; and *spatial dysgraphia* is a result of problems with spatial awareness and visual perception (Painter, 2013). Common characteristics include poor fine-motor skills, weak hand muscles, and forgetting how to form letters, shapes, and numbers. People also struggle with spacing letters, words, and numbers, which leads to illegible handwriting.

When working with a child who has been diagnosed with dysgraphia, the school occupational therapist is a valuable resource. Children who struggle with their writing are often very self-aware that they are performing below their peers, so be cautious about displaying their written work. Research shows that dysgraphia can lead a child to develop anxiety and try to avoid written tasks, which can affect the child's behavior and academic development (Gargot et al., 2020). Because children with writing disabilities may have weak hand muscles or must focus harder to accomplish the same amount as their peers, they may need writing breaks, a copy of class notes, or extra time to complete written tasks.

The following are some accommodations and modifications to try.

- **Access speech-to-text technology:** This technology allows children to speak into a microphone on a computer or tablet, and the device will write for them. Children can express their ideas without limitations. When I allow my seven- and eight-year-old students to use this technology, I am always amazed at the depth and creativity of their thoughts compared to what they are able to write with pencil and paper. This method also works well when answering brief questions on Google Forms. (I switch between paper and technology to expose them to both options.)

- **Use typing:** Start teaching children how to type by allowing them time to use child-friendly computer typing programs, such as Type to Learn (for children ages six to twelve) and Type to Learn Jr. and Dance Mat

Typing (for ages six to eight). There are cute online typing games for preschoolers and typing activities and lessons for different age groups. Some schools build time into the weekly schedule for children to learn keyboarding skills; other classrooms can develop their own schedule for teaching children these skills or offer it as an option in a center.

- **Use paper with raised lines:** This type of paper works well for printing letters, numbers, and words. Children can feel the lines while they write. Provide model letters and numbers and scaffold their writing by breaking it into manageable steps.

- **Provide a slanted board:** A slanted board makes writing easier. I provide a DIY example on page 128.

- **Try specialized pencils and grips:** These tools help children hold the utensil correctly, which will improve their writing.

Children Performing Well Below Expectations

Each child is unique in their needs and abilities. Be careful not to separate children because they are performing well below their peers or appear to have special needs. Depending on the early childhood program, children can receive extra services while attending school with their peers. All children benefit from friendships; peer models for learning academic, problem-solving, and social skills; improved language experiences; and higher expectations. When children with learning differences are included, their peers gain friendships, learn to understand differences more, and enjoy helping their friends when they encounter obstacles (Department of Children and Families, 2022). They develop compassion and discover that children with lower performance or special needs are more similar to them than they are different (Croft, 2017). Whole inclusion plants seeds of compassion and understanding that continue to grow as the children develop into more empathic adults.

Accommodations and Modifications

For struggling children, even without any diagnosis, there are many ways teachers can support them at school. Visuals will help with language delays and understanding concepts. Provide directions in clear and concise language and provide a safe and nurturing learning environment. Help with friendship skills by using social stories and role-playing, along with peers of the same age, to learn appropriate friendship skills.

Reduce demands and adjust the curriculum to meet the individual child's needs (Hughes, 2006). Children struggling may need information presented to them in various ways over time to gain new skills. By providing multiple methods of representation, action, and expression, and various means of engagement, UDL works well for children of all ability levels. Teachers face a delicate balance between giving children the support they need and gradually reducing the number of prompts and accommodations to build independence.

Some students may also qualify for an Individual Education Plan (IEP) or Individualized Family Service Plan (IFSP), which is a plan that focuses on goals and ways to help the child and track their progress.

Talented Children or Outside-the-Box Thinkers

Children have a wide range of abilities, and some children who catch on quickly or have certain talents need opportunities to expand their learning. They do not need to be officially identified as "gifted" to benefit from additional challenges while they learn. For example, a child may come to preschool knowing all the letters of the alphabet and ready to learn letter sounds. The child is ready for the next level. Consider ways to extend lessons for children as they work toward becoming expert learners.

Talented students often start showing their skills at a young age. It might be a few years before they are identified. Still, teachers can begin making accommodations to support them right away. According to the National Association for Gifted Children, gifted students can achieve at higher levels when compared with their peers in one or more domains. Like other children with learning variabilities, they need accommodations and modifications at school to succeed (National Association for Gifted Children, n.d.).

UDL is for all learners in the classroom, regardless of their abilities. Talented children sometimes need accommodations, too, yet are often overlooked. According to Dr. Temple Grandin, it is possible for some areas of the brain to have multiple connections and other regions of the brain to have few connections (Grandin and Panek, 2013). How the brain is wired affects a child's skills and may result in uneven skill levels. For example, a child may be able to read words in preschool but unable to recognize any numbers. Sometimes, children with special needs are left out of the gifted-and-talented programs, even though they may have one or more areas in which they are gifted.

Accommodations can include a classroom library with books at a variety of reading levels, so children can have opportunities to use their skills to read. Teachers can use tiered assignments by starting with a goal, designing the lesson with low, middle, and high levels for students to choose from. Scaffolding can be helpful for struggling students. Surprisingly, some struggling students put forth extra effort with support to reach the highest level of the assignment. Learning how talented children think and utilizing their talents is essential (Kaplan Early Learning Company, n.d.).

Suppose a child has abilities in math, letters, reading, or writing abilities. In that case, she should be able to work at a higher level and not be expected to perform well below her capabilities simply because particular skills are taught at that grade level.

Dual Language Learners

Young children who speak a language other than English at home and are learning English in the educational setting are referred to as dual language learners (DLLs) (Irwin, 2017). Accommodations and modifications will depend on the individual child's ability and level in learning English. Many accommodations that work well for students with disabilities are also helpful for DLL students. If you are teaching in the early elementary space, your English as a second language (ESL) teacher is an excellent resource.

Something as simple as a translation app can be a useful accommodation. For example, the Google Translate app allows you to converse with someone who speaks a different language and instantly translates and puts what they say on the phone screen. Then, you can hand the phone to them, and they can talk, translating into your language. You can go back and forth and have a conversation. This app or similar technology may be beneficial when meeting with parents or working children who do not speak English.

In addition, accommodations listed for children with hearing impairments can work well for DLLs: use visuals, provide clear and concise directions, and model examples for the children. And make your classroom culturally welcoming. For example, display posters and provide books in the children's home languages. Ask the families to loan cultural artifacts and to share music or stories with the children.

Children in Poverty

Poverty may not sound like something that goes with UDL, yet studies and data show a correlation between children who live in poverty and lower academic performance. Between children in poverty and those not living in poverty, significant income-based achievement gaps have been shown in scores for math and reading tests (Ladd, 2012). All children have equal rights to access an education without barriers. If a child does not have their basic needs met, they have a significant obstacle to learning. For example, a student may arrive at school hungry. A child may need medical care. A child may not have access to books and other learning experiences at home. A child may lack supervision after school or access to warm winter clothing.

> A six-year-old in a school where I worked wore the same dirty outfit for a couple of weeks in a row. He also had significant behavior problems. I noticed that he was the same size as my son, so I brought some clothes in one day and asked him before class if he wanted to switch to clean clothes. The change was immediate. He walked back into our classroom like a million dollars and had fewer behavior incidents that day, which I had not expected. His clothing had been an obstacle to his learning. After that, I made sure he had clean clothes for the rest of the school year. I reached out to his family's social worker and learned more about the challenges they were facing. I worked with the social worker and the child's mother, and our family fostered the child and his brother while their mother received the support that she needed.

> Another student I worked with, age seven, had a nonstop runny nose. I was concerned that the congestion was affecting his hearing. I kept wondering if I should intervene, and finally, I called his grandmother to see if she would be willing to take him to the doctor if I set it up. She

agreed. It turned out that she did not have a car; the transportation issue had prevented the family from getting appropriate medical care. An ear, nose, and throat specialist found that this child's ear drums were so infected that the doctor said fungus was growing in his ears. The child also failed a hearing test. Poor medical care had affected this child's education and his social-emotional growth. Imagine all the learning this child had missed over the years of not being able to hear.

Complex Health Conditions

The Centers for Disease Control and Prevention (2021) lists several common childhood conditions. Students with chronic and complex health issues face many learning obstacles, including frequent absences, poor attendance, and fatigue. Some health conditions can affect cognitive function; many do not. Sometimes, schools need to coordinate with the medical team and teachers to provide educational support at school or for homebound education (Hinton and Kirk, 2014). Parents and guardians are the best resources for information on the child's needs.

Some health-related conditions cause children to have physical disabilities that make it difficult for children to access their education. A child may use a wheelchair, walker, or cane or may struggle to get around in the classroom environment. Limited mobility can affect a child's access to classroom learning materials. Playgrounds with uneven surfaces and limited ways for students to join their peers and engage in social exchange are also a barrier for children with physical disabilities. It is best to create a physically accessible environment that children with mobility issues can easily navigate. Think about the classroom layout and set it up so walkers and wheelchairs can get around the room. Make classroom supplies and learning

materials easily accessible. If needed, provide a desk and chair that suit the child's needs. When planning a class field trip, make the travel accessible to all students.

Raise Awareness in Your Classroom and School

Spread awareness in your classroom and school about learning variabilities. Teach students to accept all children. By providing information in a positive learning environment with acceptance and understanding of the different learning variabilities, there will be fewer incidents of bullying and teasing. Support educators in understanding practical ways they can work with children with a variety of learning abilities.

Prejudice against children who are different is often the result of a lack of knowledge. Educators are already excellent at promoting kindness in the classroom; take the next step to include awareness of learning differences.

> A third-grade teacher recently shared the book *Thank You, Mr. Falker* (Polacco, 2012) with her students. This is the story of a girl who finally learns to read in fifth grade thanks to a teacher who is open to trying various methods to teach her. The third-grade teacher wanted to spread awareness in her classroom about different types of learners. When asked what they learned from the story, one student, age eight, said, "If you can't learn one way, it doesn't mean other ways won't work for learning." She understood one of the core concepts of UDL: using multiple ways to learn and show what you know.

Partnership with Parents and Guardians

As you shift the way you teach to include the UDL guidelines, keep parents and guardians in the loop on the changes you are making, and welcome their input. Educators know that parent involvement is essential to a child's education. Part of a thriving classroom atmosphere includes parents and guardians who feel their voice is heard in their child's education.

According to the article "Working with Families of Children with Special Needs" (Sefton, Gargiulo, and Graves, 1991), the success of interventions often depends on the educators' ability to work with the parents. This article suggests remembering that children with learning variabilities are more like than different from their peers. Be open to the parents' feelings, keep communication flowing, and try to share concerns in a nonthreatening manner (Sefton, Gargiulo, and Graves, 1991).

• • •

Understanding learning variabilities is key to planning innovative lesson plans and classroom environments. You can break down barriers to learning by making accommodations as accessible as pencils and paper. Provide the tools needed to empower children to be lifelong learners, and partner with families to help all children reach their potential. A UDL mindset and understanding can create a more equitable and accessible education for all children.

CHAPTER 5
Infusing Technology into the UDL Classroom

"If you design your classroom to meet everyone's needs, anyone can participate."
• **Christopher Bugaj,** *The New Assistive Tech: Making Learning Awesome for All!* •

Low, medium, and high tech can reduce barriers in the classroom and empower children to be expert learners. You do not need to be a tech expert to include a few fundamental changes in your lessons. Even small changes will offer benefits that go far beyond the classroom. Technology integration enhances or makes learning more interactive. For example, suppose children are learning about rhyming words. An interactive smartboard activity that matches pictures of rhyming words could be an effective and fun part of the lesson. Another way to incorporate technology is to use multimedia when introducing a new skill. For example, in a lesson on rain forests, a virtual field trip, video clip, or slideshow would enhance the lesson and make it more engaging for children.

Technology integration is not about using the most expensive tool; it is about being aware of the range of options, then choosing the best strategy for success. Because technology is changing and evolving quickly, starting with standard technology can make incorporating UDL easier to implement.

Technology integration looks at a balance of choices and realistic goals for blending the best tools into the lesson. For example, a child with language delays may struggle to communicate what he knows at school, causing a major obstacle to learning. The option of using a communication book or tablet with pictures can allow the child to participate in class discussions and at centers with peers. Such a simple addition to the original lesson plans can dramatically affect a child's learning and social-emotional development. When they can participate, children are not left sitting, unable to participate and feeling embarrassed at their lack of skills. Instead, they feel like valued class members and can be more independent and rely less on adult support (Hecker et al., 2002). With technology, children can create, discover, learn from digital content as well as easily use assistive features and supports.

Technology offers benefits for educators too. Teachers can share content with children and colleagues. They can teach both in person and virtually. Teachers can attend workshops and classes that would not have been possible before. Technology has opened many doors and removed barriers to learning. In the following sections, we take a look at steps for infusing technology into the UDL classroom:

- **T:** Target child and educator needs.

- **E:** Examine the technology choices. What tools are available and applicable?

- **C:** Create opportunities to integrate technology. How can the educator implement UDL with the help of technology in the classroom?

- **H:** Handle the implementation and monitor children's learning, plan, teach, assess, gather data, reflect, and adjust.

T: Target Student and Educator Needs

The first step in integrating technology in the UDL classroom is to conduct a needs assessment to determine how technology could help bridge the gap and make learning more equitable. There are many ways to conduct a needs assessment, but generally, the process involves four main steps.

1. Conduct a student needs assessment to create a technology integration profile for each child (National Center for Education Statistics, n.d.).

2. Investigate the results and prioritize (National Center for Education Statistics, n.d.).

3. Conduct an educator needs assessment. For example, does the educator need additional training to use a method or device that would be helpful to the child's learning? (Ileto, 2019).

4. Assess, take data, reflect, and adjust. It is best to have an ongoing needs assessment as the instruction and children's needs change.

Conduct a Student Needs Assessment

For each child, create a technology-integration profile. Note any specialized programs, such as the child's IEP or 504 plan, and any other services, such as an advanced-learners program or DLL support. Create a list of the child's learning variabilities, strengths and weaknesses, and current level of performance. A needs assessment called the Student, Environment, Tasks, and Tools (SETT) is useful for this purpose (Hollingshead, Zabala, and Carson, 2022).

- **Student:** Examine the child's current performance levels in academic, social, communication, vision, hearing, mobility, and daily living skills.

- **Environment:** Investigate the classroom arrangement, the materials used, and how instruction is delivered. As explained in chapter 2, the environment can play a huge role in a child's learning.

- **Tasks for learning:** What tasks are essential for the child to be able to accomplish? Depending on the tasks and goals for the lesson, it will make a difference in what tech tools would be helpful if needed.

- **Tools for learning:** What tools are currently being used, and what additional tools would be helpful? Consider the options of low, middle, or high tech that could be incorporated to make learning more accessible. If the child is doing a project with glue, scissors, and paper, the teacher may give the students a few low-tech tools to make it easier. Examples could include adapted scissors to make cutting easier, disposable gloves to keep sensory-sensitive hands clean when using the glue, and highlighted lines to make them more visible on the paper for cutting.

The following chart is an example of how the SETT can be used.

Student	Environment	Tasks	Tools
• Age five • Can hold various writing utensils but can only scribble on a paper • Cannot print their name, letters, or numbers	Kindergarten classroom	Fine-motor tasks: drawing and writing	• Adaptive writing utensils such as wider crayons, markers, or pencils • Soft grips to go on pencils or grips with guides for holding a pencil • Pencils with different shapes that are easier for small hands to hold • Wooden letters, numbers, and shapes for tracing • Slant board to make printing easier • Special raised line paper to make it easier for a child to feel • Color-coded paper with top, middle, and bottom lines • Apps to practice tracing letters, shapes, and numbers • Speech-to-text software after they start to write beginning sentences

Looking at this child's age, tasks, and tools, the educator can recommend what to try first to help the student succeed. I usually start with a low-tech intervention and see if that is enough support for the child to be successful. Then, if needed, I move to higher tech.

Investigate the Results and Prioritize

Once you have the needs assessments, you can create a technology-integration profile with the best choices for each child. (We examine different types of technology later in this chapter.) Although it would be great to include all areas that would be helpful, it is more realistic to prioritize and start with the most critical needs. Many children may benefit from noise-cancellation headphones, wiggle seats, special writing utensils, a slanted board for writing, or additional classroom visuals, but there may not be funds to do it all. Consider the learning goals and the funds available to purchase assistive technology and then plan by prioritizing. One year, I made slant boards, which make forming letters, numbers, or words easier, because writing was one of the greatest struggles of my small group. Another year, my students were struggling with understanding vocabulary and having difficulty with comprehension. So, I made adaptive books with additional visuals to use when reading with that group. A few years ago, we needed more e-readers and e-books for guided reading groups, so I wrote a grant to acquire those tools. The first- and second-graders found the e-readers to be highly engaging and they were able to customize the font size and background color to make it easier to read.

Conduct an Educator Needs Assessment

This assessment is vital to pinpoint areas where the teacher may need additional professional development to implement technology successfully. Decide which technology tools can be used immediately and which must wait until the educator has further training. For example, if the teacher is familiar with Chromebooks, that tool use could start in September. If the district is offering training on smartboards in October, the educator may wait to use that tech tool until after the training. Like their students, teachers need different levels of support to be successful in using technology and integrating it into the lessons. Often districts buy technology without offering training and support for their staff. The needs assessment is helpful in targeting professional development that is relevant for staff.

Assess, Gather Data, Reflect, and Adjust

Once you choose a technological tool, pay attention to who uses it, how well children are able to use it, whether or not it meets the intended goals, and how you may need to adjust. Do the children need more training on the tool before the next lesson? Were the tech choices helpful for child success, or should a different type of tech be used the next time? Reflection and data are crucial to ensure the tech matches a child's changing needs. I will sometimes try something new and then find out that what I thought would work well with particular children didn't work for them after all.

I keep records on the types of technology that I use with different children. For example, I have tried different types of math-fluency programs to see which ones help children learn their basic math facts better. I keep notes on how well the children are able to interact with the program and whether it actually helps them learn math facts. Because of this data, I have dropped one of the math programs and kept the program that showed more progress.

E: Examine the Technology Choices

Many types of technology can enhance a child's education and allow for more independence. For example, if a child holds a pencil with his fist, a simple pencil grip or a different type of writing utensil might help him learn to hold writing instruments with his fingers. If a child has trouble remembering the steps for washing hands, then a visual strip of pictures placed at the child's level by the sink can serve as a reminder. If a child is struggling to learn his letters, using a letter game on a tablet can give him more practice in a highly engaging way. If a child struggles with behavior at recess, visual schedule of ideas for things to do outside can help. I have provided step stools for children who are small for their age and cannot touch the floor when they sit at a table. The goal is to build independence and success. Technology doesn't have to be high tech to make a difference for a child.

If you work in a school district, contact the assistive technology consultant and school technology coordinator to find out what tech is available. Many communities have school technology support that could be an asset in finding out this information. Some districts offer support in writing lesson plans and helping in the classroom during a lesson on integrating technology. Educators can also look at the national technology standards (available at https://www.iste.org/iste-standards) for additional ideas. Preschool teachers can contact their area education centers and child-care resource and referral agency to find support for assistive technology for their students.

C: Create Opportunities to Integrate Technology

Teachers can plan to integrate technology throughout the learning process. The SAMR model is one way to do this. SAMR stands for substitution, augmentation, modification, and redefinition.

- **Substitution:** This involves switching a traditional delivery method for tech without changing the content, such as typing a story on a word processor instead of drafting it with pencil and paper, or reading an e-book instead of a paper book. It can also be a different way for teachers to teach a lesson.

- **Augmentation:** At this level of support, the content stays the same, but how students interact with learning is exchanged for the same skills using technology. For example, it could be a digital rather than a paper test. Or it could be content language support including visuals or definitions for part of the content. Interactive resources such as the children's visual and auditory encyclopedia PebbleGo can be a way to learn about a specific topic. Young children could trace letters and numbers on a tablet instead of on paper or use a tablet for communication instead of using a picture communication book.

- **Modification:** Modification is a significant redesign of the lesson material using technology. For example, a teacher could introduce an investigation of coral reefs by putting Google Earth on the smartboard and zooming in to view the Great Barrier Reef or showing the children a slideshow on coral-reef animals. To share their learning, children might create a multimedia presentation instead of writing a report. If a child has serious issues with fine-motor skills, he could use assistive technology to work with virtual math manipulatives instead of plastic ones.

- **Redefinition:** Redefinition allows children to have experiences that otherwise would not be possible (Terada, 2020). Students can learn through interactive technology, such as taking virtual field trips, viewing or creating multimedia presentations, or making virtual author visits. They can also learn in ways that are not available without technology, such as through using robots or computers.

Technology integration benefits all students. Social-emotional skills grow as children work together while using a tablet. Fine-motor skills develop as children learn to swipe, trace, and manipulate interactive learning games. Technology helps to teach children how to follow multistep directions. Children are often engaged when interacting with a smartboard during a lesson; even my students who are usually off task are focused. And technology makes learning fun.

Learning has changed from the traditional classroom model to a blended learning model, with technology and traditional methods incorporated into a powerful combination. The International Society for Technology in Education (ISTE) has developed education and technology standards to help students and teachers thrive in today's technological age. The standards are a great resource to help educators integrate technology into the classroom with high-quality modeling and teaching.

After deciding what the children's needs are and understanding the types of technology available, the next step is to look at the lesson goals to find the best ways to integrate technology.

For example, in an early childhood classroom, children might play with robots to learn about coding. They discover that the robots move only when a child uses the green tactile arrows to build paths for them. They build communication skills as they work with peers to decide what a robot should do next (Granone and Reikerås, 2021). The more the children explore and play, the more they develop problem-solving skills, language, and social skills.

H: Handle the Implementation and Monitor Student Learning

Part of helping students and educators succeed with technology is to train them to use it. School districts often purchase technology and place it in the classroom without the proper training. The technology will then sit unused or underused beneath its full potential. Children and teachers have a wide range of experiences with technology, so training is essential to allow them to see the possibilities.

A kindergarten class I worked with had a digital microscope hooked to the classroom computer. As they explored the technology, the children discovered more uses for it. The more they investigated, the more they learned and shared. Their excitement was evident as they gained additional skills. For example, they discovered that the digital microscope could take pictures. They made pictures of slides that they then enlarged on the computer screen. Because the Lego center was near the computers, they decided to take family pictures of the Lego people, which was hilarious. They saved these images in the program, which allowed everyone to see them when it was their turn on the microscope. This encouraged other children to try all the different ways slides could be observed. They had so much fun learning valuable skills, which they later applied when we started a science unit using the digital microscope.

STUDENT SAFETY AND CONFIDENTIALITY

When using technology connected to the internet, it is essential to consider safety and confidentiality. Follow your school and district guidelines. Always have parental permission for students to access online educational digital content and consent for videos or digital portfolios. Remember the Family Educational Rights and Privacy Act (FERPA) when sharing student information and files with other teachers. You can learn more about FERPA here: https://www2.ed.gov/policy/gen/guid/fpco/ferpa/index.html

An advantage of technology is the many ways it allows communication between school and home. The school website can have a wealth of information and resources for parents. In addition, individual classroom websites can share important dates and homework and highlight student work (with permission). Educators can write classroom blogs that they can share with families. Virtual meetings can allow parents to participate in discussions with teachers or easily share student progress and work electronically. The Google Translate app can translate live while communicating with a parent who is learning English as a second language.

Another way to communicate is by creating digital portfolios of each student, with videos of them reading, writing, or completing math, along with pictures of their work, tests, and more. Digital portfolios offer a greater perspective of the whole child than a test score alone. The portfolios shared at parent conferences or IEP meetings allow families to see their children learning at school.

As educators prepare children to become life-long learners, technology makes content more engaging and accessible while encouraging collaboration and critical thinking. It does not have to be expensive or complicated to break down barriers and help students learn. Many modern tech devices and programs have built-in, easy-to-access accommodations.

Educators can design, develop, and infuse technology into the UDL classroom by targeting student needs, examining technology choices, and creating opportunities to integrate technology. Creating assistive tech profiles for each student helps educators decide what tech tools would be the most effective for student achievement and make learning more accessible and equitable.

Technology also supports teachers in making more engaging and interactive lessons, assessing student learning, and tracking student progress. In addition, teachers can use technology to communicate with families, meet virtually, create classroom websites, and collaborate with other educators. The most crucial aspect of technology integration into the classroom is for students to access learning in ways that otherwise may have been impossible.

CHAPTER 6
Lesson Planning and UDL

"Students vary on many dimensions of learning, just like they vary on dimensions of size."

• **Todd Rose, developmental psychologist** •

In his 2013 TEDxTalk, "The Myth of Average," Todd Rose spoke about how the designs of Air Force jets compare to design in a classroom. He related that jets in the 1940s incorporated the latest engineering to meet the needs of the average pilot, yet many jets were crashing even with experienced pilots in the cockpit. In 1950, Lt. Gilbert S. Daniels conducted a study of 4,063 pilots. He measured their height and other body measurements in an effort to design a better jet; he was searching for data on the "average" pilot. How many of the 4,063 pilots fit the supposed average? None! Daniels found that pilots, like all humans, vary widely across dimensions. Daniels's research changed how jets are engineered to accommodate a range of sizes. This approach has allowed for a remarkably diverse pilot program in the United

States because the seats and controls can adjust for people of all sizes, allowing a variety of pilots to reach and see what they need to fly the jet (Rose, 2013).

The classroom setting is similar. For years, our curriculum and teaching methods have focused on the myth of the average student. Research shows that our brains are as different as our fingerprints (Geneux, 2021). If we continue to use traditional teaching methods, we are essentially teaching to no one. Think about that for a minute. Educators and curriculum designers have spent years focusing on the average child, who does not exist.

Instead of fitting the students to meet the curriculum, UDL encourages planning with many variables in mind. The planning includes considering the outer limits to transform the curriculum to meet a wide range of student needs. Educators can modify any lesson plan or curriculum to meet a broader range of abilities within the classroom. More than simple differential instruction, UDL asks educators to consider both their current and future students (Snelling, 2021).

Implementing UDL means teachers see students along a range of learner diversity, and children are encouraged to take an active role in their learning. Educators focus on providing a learning atmosphere and materials that capitalize on children's strengths regardless of their abilities (Pisha and Coyne, 2001).

Five Steps to UDL Lesson Planning

Think back to the UDL guidelines and fundamental principles from chapter 2.

1. **Step 1:** Examine the targeted goal.
2. **Step 2:** Consider the range of needs in the classroom and decide what types of scaffolding or adjustments would allow more children to succeed.
3. **Step 3:** Gather knowledge on the available materials, equipment, and tech.
4. **Step 4:** Use the UDL guidelines to guide the planning, teaching, and assessment choices.
5. **Step 5:** Plan, teach, assess, track data, reflect, and adjust.

Step 1: Examine the Targeted Goal

The best practice is to create a SMART goal, one that is specific or strategic, measurable, attainable, relevant, or realistic, and time bound.

- **Strategic/Specific:** Most states have objectives for each age level. The learning goal needs to be specific so that anyone reading the goal will know what is expected. Break the larger goal into specific steps for each child to take to reach the goal. For example, a short-term goal might be, "The students will be able to recognize the letters and sounds for *M, T, F, H,* and *A* by the end of September with 80 percent accuracy through one-on-one assessment with the teacher or paraprofessional teacher."

  The long-term goal is for the children to recognize all the letters and sounds of the alphabet by the end of the school year. Knowing whether children have reached the target will be challenging if the goal is not specific. Breaking the goals into measurable steps will help track student progress toward recognizing all alphabet letters and sounds.

- **Measurable:** How will the educator know the children have accomplished each specific goal? Goals must be measurable, so the teacher can collect data and know what skills require additional instruction. So, back to our specific short-term goal: "The students will be able to recognize the letters and sounds for *M, T, F, H,* and *A* by the end of September with 80 percent accuracy through one-on-one assessment with the teacher or paraprofessional teacher." The percentage of accuracy allows the teacher to measure how many students meet the short-term goal and to adjust instruction as needed to help any child who needs additional support.

- **Attainable/Achievable:** Next, consider whether the goal is possible within the wide range of student needs. Knowing your class, can they all learn the target letters by the end of September? Would scaffolding, accommodations, or tiered instruction allow more children to reach the goal? Do some students need to have additional small-group time to work on the letters? What prerequisite skills are essential for the targeted goal? The goal might be appropriate for the age group, but after reviewing the student profiles and data, the teacher may need to teach prerequisite skills first. Small groups of children may need extra work on specific skills to be able to attempt the next goal. For example, the data shows that five out of the twenty children in the class still need to reach mastery of letter recognition of the specific goal. Reteaching using a different approach may be required for all the children to gain mastery. During center rotations, when the teacher has small-group time, she can work with the small group to target missing skills. During classroom independent time, the teacher might pull a quick, targeted group together to help them to bridge the gap.

Another way to bridge that gap is by using technology. There are learning programs for most skills being taught in early childhood. Children who need extra practice could have fifteen to twenty minutes on the computer or tablet to work on specific skills. Some school districts have programs they recommend and a subscription or membership so children can access them. For example, our school has Reading A–Z, which is a subscription site for working on beginning phonics and reading. There are also fun and interactive apps children can use to work on basic skills. It is best to experiment with different apps or learning websites to see which ones work for the skills you want to teach. Technology is highly motivating for most children and will repeat the same skill as long as is needed.

- **Realistic/Relevant:** What sounds good on paper may not work in the classroom. This is why checking for possible barriers and knowing the student profiles is essential. Does the goal align with the state, school, or national standards? Is the goal realistic for your students? For example, look at our specific goal for letter and sound recognition. The kindergarten state objective may be for children to learn letters and sounds. However, your student profiles show that most children need more exposure to books and letters. In that case, start with a goal that aligns with the children's needs and work toward the state standards.

- **Time-bound:** When does the educator plan to teach the goal, and when should the students show mastery of the goal? It is important to put a specific time frame for mastery, to know if the students have met the goal. If the time frame is left off, educators will not know whether the children should know the letters by the end of kindergarten or by the end of second grade. The amount of time will depend on the learning variabilities in the classroom, teacher expectations, and district timelines (O'Neill, Conzemius, Commodore, and Pulsfus, 2006).

Step 2: Consider the Range of Needs and Choose Types of Scaffolding or Adjustments

The range of needs refers to the different learning variabilities in the classroom. For example, would active children benefit from standing while they work? Are there children with cognitive delays who might need additional support? Would some children benefit from visual steps to help them while working toward the goal? The teacher gathers all this information and puts different choices into the lesson. The idea is to plan for a range and then allow students to have options. Sometimes, they need guidance in making choices. Still, in time, they will realize that accommodations and assistive technology are available for them to use. Often, what is planned for a few children helps other children too. For example, you might have noise-cancellation headphones because you know that one child has sensory issues. Still, other children who are easily distracted or do not like noise may also benefit from that option. Having readily available assistive technology removes the stigma of the items being for "special needs." Instead, they become tools for success.

Providing scaffolding and multilevel instruction empowers more students to reach the lesson goal. What kinds of barriers might affect the achievement of the targeted goal? The learning variabilities will help you decide which adjustments may be needed. For example, if a child is advanced in a subject, they will need extended learning to reach their potential fully. Another child may benefit from additional visuals or other accommodations to succeed. Many low-, medium-, and high-tech tools are available to help level the playing field for students while learning. Sometimes, a low- or medium-tech item, such as an adaptive writing utensil or noise-canceling headphones, are enough for a child to be successful with the lesson. Other times a child may benefit from a high-tech item, such as an app for a tablet, to work on the goal.

When the educator inputs the goal into their plans, the next step is to consider the different routes students could take to reach the goal. One child may learn that a specific way works well for them; another child may find a way that does not work for them, but next time they might make a different choice. Trial and error is an essential part of their learning process.

Let's consider a kindergarten classroom and some ways that the teacher plans for barriers and adjusts instruction. The teacher asks the children how to make the letter *M*. One child chooses a slant board to make writing more accessible. A couple of children decide to use the adapted writing utensils. A few children are writing on paper with crayons, and another is tracing the letter on a tablet. Yet another child needs hand-over-hand teacher support to make the letter. Everyone works with their peers, and no one is left out. The assistive technology is readily available to anyone to choose. Everyone will arrive at the target goal. The difference is the amount of scaffolding or accommodations needed along the way. With flexibility and choices, all students have a chance to be successful with the same goal.

Step 3: Gather Knowledge on Available Materials, Equipment, and Technology

Consider the areas where adjustments might be possible, including instructional methods, assignments, assessments, and environment. Then, proactively plan for barriers in advance. One way to adjust instruction is to examine the children's learning profiles and look for possible obstacles. If some children struggle with auditory directions, the teacher can adjust her plans to add more visuals. Knowing that multiple means of representation help children learn, the teacher decides to vary how the lessons are presented to include different modalities to reach more children.

Some of the barriers for three- to five-year-olds include the following:

- **Poor fine-motor skills or weak hand muscles:** A child with poor fine-motor skills may need accommodations with different writing utensils, adaptive scissors, or extra teacher support when completing projects or activities.

- **Speech and language delays:** Children with speech and language delays may benefit from having a picture communication book, additional visuals in the classroom, and plenty of opportunities to use language throughout their school day through songs, rhymes, and center time with peers. If they have significant language delays, they may also benefit from devices or apps with pictures for communication.

- **Physical or mobility issues:** Children with physical or mobility challenges need a well-laid-out classroom to access everything they need independently.

- **Lack of exposure to books and learning materials:** Some children may arrive at preschool or kindergarten with a different exposure to books and learning materials than their peers. They might not know how to hold a book, crayon, or scissors. They would benefit from more opportunities to explore the different learning materials and books.

Possible barriers for six- to eight-year-olds include the following:

- **Speech and language delays:** Speech and language issues can affect reading and writing at this age. Children usually write the same as they can talk, so delays in talking affect writing. Reading and learning phonics are affected because children need to hear the differences in sounds to build reading and phonics fluency and comprehension and understanding of language.

- **Fine-motor skills:** At this age, weak fine-motor skills can interfere with keeping up with their peers in reading, writing, and math. This is because children are expected to start writing beginning sentences, numbers, and letters at this age. Some interventions include the use of a slanted desk, adaptive writing utensils, options to use speech-to-text, or opportunities to tell their answers verbally. They may also benefit from activities that can strengthen hand muscles, including using playdough or doing any activity that could build hand muscles.

Work with the school team to create a list of materials, equipment, curriculum, tech tools or software, assistive tech, and manipulatives that are available. It is also helpful to have a list of people in supportive positions who are available to help. For example, math and reading coaches, special education team members, ELL staff, and other specialty areas can support teachers when planning. Frequently, the district also has staff to support the classroom when needed. Resources within a school or district often go unused because only some know what is available, or an educator needs more training or support to use the resources effectively. School-wide staff development is a good time for the different specialty areas and district leaders to share available resources and offer additional training.

Step 4: Use the UDL Guidelines to Guide Planning, Teaching, and Assessment Choices

Recall from chapter 2 the discussion on providing multiple means of engagement, representation, and action and expression. The goal is to have expert learners who are purposeful and motivated, resourceful and knowledgeable, and strategic and goal directed (CAST, 2022b). Consider flexibility and scaffolding during student learning, assessment, and feedback as you choose how to provide multiple ways for children to engage with the learning topic.

Multiple means of engagement: The lesson will start with teaching using multiple means of engagement, which help children to connect to learning and the world around them. Activate the children's brains by getting them excited about learning the lesson using what you know about each student's learning profile, barriers, and the SMART goal. Connect to prior knowledge and let students know the lesson's purpose. Present key concepts using visuals, anchor charts, or hands-on materials and manipulatives to give children ways to engage in the lesson through multiple formats. It might be a puppet, song, or high-interest book for younger children to introduce the lesson. For older students, it could be a short video clip, slides, anchor charts, and interactive learning through an online interactive question game for teachers and students such as Kahoot or other formats. Once the students are hooked and listening, they are more likely to retain the information. We have all sat through boring lessons or accidentally taught them ourselves, so we know that boredom or lack of enthusiasm for learning is the fastest way to lose your students and set off behavior issues.

Multiple means of representation: Engage the representation area of the brain, which stores and sorts information into categories. Provide various instructional materials to support learning during independent practice and small-group learning. Provide and guide students with appropriate accommodations, assistive technology, and learning materials as needed. For example, students may interact with manipulatives, smartboards, projects, books, and other learning materials designated by the teacher and the lesson to work towards their learning goals and objectives.

Multiple means of action and representation: Next, provide multiple means of action and expression, activating the brain's strategic networks. Providing options and various pathways for engagement stimulates student interest. Some methods include interactive smartboard activities, apps, multimedia, computer activities, manipulatives, and experiments. Take data and provide time for reflection and feedback (Burns and Church, 2021).

Step 5: Plan, Teach, Assess, Track Data, Reflect, and Adjust

The best practice for any teaching method is a cycle of planning, teaching, assessing, tracking data, reflecting, and adjusting. These steps are essential when using the UDL methods to decide what works best and what areas need adjustment. It is also vital for teachers and children to reflect on the lesson and consider future improvements. Students' voices are an integral part of UDL instruction because they can provide valuable feedback on the beneficial aspects of the lesson and what would work better to help them learn.

ASSESSMENT

Many educators must adhere to district guidelines on assessment. Unfortunately, current assessments are designed with few options for learners to show what they know or are written in such a way that they are tricky for a child to answer. This is especially true when children are in kindergarten and older, but preschools can also struggle with assessment regulations. As much as possible, consider a variety of assessment options, such as rating scales, portfolios, observations, checklists, norm-referenced tests, interviews with the child, allowing the child to point to responses, and short video clips of the child completing the task or goal. Try to use assessments that keep the goal and expectations the same but allow children a variety of ways to show what they know.

For example, if a preschool class is learning shapes, the teacher might assess children's understanding by circling all the triangles. The assessment can vary by allowing a child with poor motor skills to point to the triangles instead. For a child who is delayed in her academic skills, the assessment might ask them to match shapes instead of finding specific shapes or to choose the triangles from a group of shape manipulatives. A child who is advanced might be asked to label the shapes in a group of manipulatives or to find more than one type of triangle.

Digital portfolios are another way for children to show what they know. Portfolios can address the main parts of the goal and work well with the UDL teaching methods. For example, for children who are learning letter sounds, the teacher could record short video clips of each child saying the sounds that letters represent. A portfolio allows the teacher to see the progress over time, with information such as samples from the child's work, notes about the instruction rate, an interview, observation, and tests. Portfolios can include print material, digital images, and even videos. A video of a child engaged in math, science, reading, or writing can show the steps she is taking and places where the child needs support or more advanced work.

Typically, a teacher takes notes when a child reads and works on beginning phonics skills, to note which words, letters, or sounds have errors or need additional teaching. Although this is excellent data, when a teacher videos while taking data, the educator can see what the child is doing during the assessment, which may or may not affect the child's scores. For example, I filmed each child while they read for one minute, and I took a running record to check their reading fluency. Later during my planning time, I looked at the videos and compared the children's final scores with what I could see on the video. One student kept looking around the room and asking me random questions about the passage. Even with prompts, this continued. His fluency score was lower than when I last tested him, but this wasn't due to student error. The film clearly showed the child could read but spent too much time off task. Videos can also show if children have confidence while reading or if they slowly sound out each word they read correctly.

I have found that sharing digital portfolios at parent-teacher conferences is one of the most effective methods for communicating children's learning with families. Videos show the progress that test scores alone cannot. For example, I recently shared a digital portfolio with a family who was concerned their child hadn't progressed in reading because all the child's grade-level reading tests remained low. I showed a video of the student reading the first week of school and one I had taken more recently. The recent video clearly showed that the child had made tremendous progress over the year. Unfortunately, testing on grade-level tests remains low because, despite all the gains, the child is still below her peers. The digital portfolio can show progress that does not appear on age or grade-level assessments.

Younger children might be close to mastering their letter sounds but still make some errors when saying them. A video of the child telling the sounds will show she is making progress, even if the assessment still indicates that she is missing many letter sounds. A child with a language delay could demonstrate an understanding of concepts through painting, drawing, or writing answers. Children could do projects to demonstrate their knowledge and skills. For example, in a science investigation into the concepts of living and nonliving, they could cut out pictures from magazines for each category and make a poster to show their understanding.

Presentations are another highly motivating way to assess children's abilities; I have used this with ages five and up. They can learn how to use introductory Google slides or PowerPoint with pictures or pictures with words, depending on their age, to create a presentation on the topic.

After a science unit on beginning weather, I gave the children choices of creating slides or posters, verbally naming the four vocabulary terms and their meanings, or answering the same questions on paper. I gave them a visual rubric, showed examples of each choice, and let them pick. I supported them as needed and used a rubric for grading. Flexibility and choices allow children to become more independent and feel in control of their learning.

According to Brookhart (2013), a good rubric must include measures that are appropriate, definable, observable, distinct from one another, complete, and able to support descriptions along a continuum of quality. Performance rubrics should be descriptive and clear, cover the whole range of performance, distinguish among levels, center the target performance, and feature parallel descriptions from level to level (Brookhart, 2013). The following are simple rubrics for evaluating number recognition and early writing skills.

Rubric for Number Recognition 1–10

Skill or Goal	Not Yet	In Progress	Mastered
Recognize numbers 1–10	Recognizes three or fewer numbers	Recognizes four to six numbers	Recognizes numbers 1–10

Rubric for First-Grade Writing

Skill or Goal	Not Yet	In Progress	Mastered
Starts three sentences with a capital letter	No capital letters at the start of the sentences	One or two sentences started with capital letters	Three sentences started with capital letters
Writes legibly	Writing is illegible	Some of the words are near the lines and are legible	The letters in the words formed correctly and legibly
Puts a space between each word	All words in sentences are hooked together without spaces	Some spacing between words in the sentences	Each word in the sentences separated by spacing
Uses punctuation at the end of each sentence	No ending punctuation used	One or two sentences have ending punctuation	All three sentences have ending punctuation
Writes three sentences	Wrote zero or one sentence	Wrote two sentences	Wrote three sentences

If you must assess using a written test, children can have choices on how they test. For example, this could include allowing students to stand or have seating choices. One child might want to test in the quiet area of the classroom or while wearing noise-cancellation headphones. Another might be more relaxed with a weighted lap pad or stuffed animal for the test. Some children find classical music relaxing while they work.

After assessing the children's learning, look at the data to help you plan instruction. Include all the ways you have gathered information, such as through observation, anecdotal notes, assignments, reports, work samples, and digital portfolios.

The challenge for many teachers is finding the time to gather data, as they are always on the go. You can collect data using paper forms, or you can create digital tracking forms on platforms such as Google Forms or Microsoft Forms. Input the SMART goal, expectations, and a measure such as a percentage or a number of correct responses. Once the data form is created, it is easy to quickly fill out the form on the go using any device connected to the internet. After a few data points are entered, the teacher can click on the form to create a digital sheet, which can be used to create graphs or charts to show progress. The charts and graphs are very informative for tracking student progress and driving instruction. The forms can be shared with everyone working with a child and can be used over and over while tracking the goal. I like using digital forms because I can open the data form from any device and check a child's progress or input data.

Another excellent method for use in early childhood is the Centers for Disease Control and Prevention's (CDC's) free milestone-tracker app, "Learn the Signs. Act Early." The checklists are organized by age, starting at two months and going through five years, and by development area. Learn more at https://www.cdc.gov/ncbddd/actearly/index.html. The information allows educators and families to see if a child is on track or needs additional support. Remember, all children vary slightly in achieving milestones, but most follow a familiar path. Use these tools as a guide. If you are concerned about a child's development, share your observations with the family and encourage them to take a copy of the milestone tracking sheet to their pediatrician. Do not suggest a diagnosis; that must come from a physician. The family can choose what they want to do with the information. If they later ask how to find additional support in your city or state, be ready with resources to help them. Learn about the programs available for early childhood special-education support in your area. Early childhood teachers are often the first to notice that a child needs additional support. As I have mentioned, early interventions are critical, and a child doesn't need a diagnosis to receive support in your classroom.

REFLECTING AND ADJUSTING

Reflection and adjustment are part of all lessons and not unique to UDL. Most teachers constantly reflect and adjust, even while they teach. As mentioned earlier, the child's voice in reflection and adjustment of lessons is also an essential part of the learning process. Children often get to contribute only if they are asked a question or participate in a class discussion, but they can be empowered when they know their voice is heard and valued. Give the children opportunities to express opinions and ideas. Even at young ages, instead of waiting for the teacher to direct them, they can become proactive, advocate for themselves, and make choices (Jordan, 2022).

Methods to engage children in using their voices include the following:

- Establish relationships with them so they feel safe to share their ideas.

- Help build their language and listening skills so they understand how to share and listen.

- Model both speaking and listening skills to help teach students that both using their voice and listening is essential.

- Allow children to share prior knowledge to help them connect with the lesson (Fox, 2016).

At the National UDL Conference in August 2022, Keith Jones, a recognized leader within the social-justice and disability-rights movement, gave a powerful speech on why students' voices are so important. He talked about part of his education, of being put in a classroom away from the regular education classes from the time he was a young child because he has cerebral palsy and uses a wheelchair. Cerebral palsy affects muscles, speech, and language. People often assume because someone is in a wheelchair and struggles to speak that they also have an intellectual disability, so even though he could do more, he was often given coloring sheets or easy work during the school day.

His teacher had low expectations of what he could accomplish and did not expect him to be successful. Luckily, his mother constantly pushed for him to have equal access to education and would not let him use his disability as an excuse. He talked about having the same feelings as other children his age. Still, he felt his voice was unimportant in his education due to his disability. As heartbreaking as his story was, it was also inspirational. He eventually went to college and started a business to help others with disabilities. His message is to consider the student's voice in education and to assume that a child can be successful regardless of their disability.

Applying the Five Steps to Lesson Planning

In this section, I offer two examples of lesson planning for your consideration. The first, Teacher A, plans without using UDL methods. The second, Teacher B, uses UDL methods to inform her planning.

Teacher A without UDL Methods

This teacher has a degree in education and teaches an inclusive class of kindergartners. Among her students, one is on the autism spectrum and is sensory sensitive. One child has Down syndrome and significant language and cognitive delays. Another child has some behavior concerns, a couple of children have weak fine-motor skills, and one child already knows his shapes.

She chooses a SMART goal: The children will recognize circles, squares, rectangles, and triangles by the end of the unit. She does not consider the barriers to learning the children in her classroom face. Teacher A sets up a shapes lesson in which the children are to use sponges in the four target shapes to paint each shape on butcher paper.

The classroom falls apart quickly. The child with sensory issues is crying and refusing to touch the activity. The child with behavior issues is in and out of his seat and bothering his peers. The child with a language delay wet her pants because she couldn't tell her teacher she needed to go to the bathroom. The child who already knows these shapes finishes quickly and, without any extension ideas, is up and out of his seat. The children with weak fine-motor skills are struggling to pick up the little sponges and are becoming frustrated. The entire class is in chaos. Later, the teacher tells her colleagues that inclusion does not work, and she advocates for limiting the children who can attend the preschool.

Teacher B with UDL Methods

This teacher also has a degree in education and teaches an inclusive class of kindergartners. Among her students, one is on the autism spectrum and is sensory sensitive. One child has Down syndrome and significant language and cognitive delays. Another child has some behavior concerns, a couple of children have weak fine-motor skills, and one child already knows his shapes.

The teacher starts with a SMART goal: The children will recognize circles, squares, rectangles, and triangles by the end of the unit. During the planning, Teacher B looks at possible barriers that might hinder some children in completing the tasks and activities planned for the unit. She considers each child's learning profile and decides what each will need to be successful. She decides the lesson will use the three main UDL guidelines: multiple means of engagement, multiple means of representation, and multiple means of action and expression.

Multiple means of engagement: The unit will include different ways to gain student interest. She plans to introduce the topic by reading a story about shapes aloud during circle time. She can vary this by using an interactive digital book or an adaptive book with additional pictures, as well as with a puppet or stuffed animal.

Multiple means of representation: Each day, the teacher reinforces the names of the shapes in activities and conversations with the children. She sets up activities in the classroom in which the children can paint shapes, find shapes in the sensory table area, listen to shape stories, and sort shapes. They play an outdoor shape game and sing shape songs during transitions and at circle time.

One shapes lesson involves the children using sponges in the four shapes to sponge paint on butcher paper. She knows some children don't enjoy messy hands, so she provides disposable gloves for the children to use if they like. She also shows them how to hold a sponge with a clothespin. Keeping in mind that some children will find picking up small shapes difficult, she sets out sponge shapes in different sizes so any child who wants to use larger shapes can do so. Some of the children struggle with multistep tasks, so she provides visual steps that anyone can use. She adds these to the visuals she already provides for children who need help with requesting their needs and wants.

Multiple means of action and expression: Each day, the children have options on how they interact with the activities. They can also choose different ways to show what they know. For example, a child can point to shapes when they are named, say the names of the shapes, or draw the shapes. As an extra challenge to extend the learning, she gives the option for any child to make patterns as they sponge paint. Teacher B uses token charts for positive behavior incentives, which she originally put in place to help a child with challenging behaviors. Over time, she found that the charts work well with all her students, so they all use them.

With all the support in place, all the children can complete the activity side by side with their peers. Anyone can access the additional accommodations; they are not limited to the children the teacher had in mind when she set up the lesson. UDL is about having choices for all children and not putting any limits due to different learning variabilities. This teacher planned and taught, considering her classroom's wide range of needs.

Assess: There are many ways to assess children, including observation, anecdotal notes, assignments, reports, work samples, and digital portfolios. In this lesson, Teacher B will ask children to name the shapes while checking everyone's progress and taking notes on each child's progress. In addition to her everyday data, she can follow up by asking each child to complete additional tasks to assess their knowledge of the shapes.

Track Data: The data is tracked each day during the lesson to assess each child's progress. The teacher uses digital forms she created in advance so she can fill in the data quickly. Sometimes, she also carries a clipboard with printed data sheets that she fills out as she observes.

Reflect: The teacher reflects on what worked well for the lesson and what needs to be changed. For example, she noticed that the lesson's introduction could have been more engaging. She made a note that she would need to use a different method next time.

Adjust: The teacher takes notes on what needs to be adjusted for the next time she uses this lesson. For example, the she noticed that a couple of students seemed overwhelmed by the noise in the classroom and made a note to make the noise-cancellation headphones available as a choice for their next lesson.

When a lesson falls apart, which has happened to every teacher, it is often due to not adjusting the lesson for possible barriers or child needs during planning or classroom management. Full inclusion has many benefits, but the teacher needs training and knowledge on how to teach a range of students. Because each class is different, it takes some experimentation to find the best methods for the children you are teaching. UDL is not a magic fix, but it does offer many ways to make a classroom more engaging, which promotes higher learning and fewer behavior problems. There are still children who may need additional support beyond the regular classroom, but all other options should be considered first. When possible, the best place for children to be is in the early childhood classroom with their peers.

Supports for Different Learning Domains

Language Arts: Written Language

Many factors affect children's success in writing, including muscle strength, motivation, fine-motor skills, dysgraphia, poor spelling or reading skills, behavior challenges, and focus issues.

Children can have many options:

- Trace or write on a tablet or computer.

- Trace or write on paper with raised lines or color-coded areas to make writing multisensory and easier to see or feel.

- Use a variety of writing utensils, so even children with small hands or poor fine-motor skills can grasp, write, or draw.

- Classroom management and positive behavior interventions can encourage children to keep going and not give up.

- Use voice-to-text to type with predictive text.

Less stress must be placed on how children reach the target and more on ways to make it possible for everyone to be successful. If children feels good about themselves, they will try harder and learn additional skills. Having options will open doors for all children to reach their writing goals and beyond (Hitchcock, Meyer, Rose, and Jackson, 2002).

Even though writing in school has been limited to paper and pencil for many years, with technological advances, we have leveled the playing field for students with learning variabilities and allowed them to have opportunities that were not available years ago. My grandmother graduated from college in 1918 and taught for seven years. At that time, teachers could not continue to teach after marriage, so when she married my grandfather, she had to quit teaching. We would consider that crazy today, yet many teaching methods she used in the early 1900s still exist. It is time to match our current brain research, knowledge of learning variabilities, and modern technology when planning to include all children.

> During writing lessons, John, age eight, would cry, hide under his desk, scribble on his paper, and do anything but complete the writing assignment. He could verbally tell story ideas, but getting words on paper was a struggle that took an excessive amount of time.
>
> One day, his attitude changed when the children were offered a choice between writing with paper and pencil or using a word processor to compose a story. Instead of having a meltdown, John was motivated to type. He had fun writing a short story that he could not wait to share. His problem was not that he could not write; he simply struggled if writing was limited to paper and pencil.

Language Arts: Reading

A number of tools can help children who are struggling with learning to read.

- **Text-to-speech:** For children who are below grade level in reading, built-in accommodations allow a computer or tablet to read the on-screen text aloud. This method would enable a child to actively participate in a research project with their classmates (Wood, 2001).

- **Software:** Struggling readers are often limited in what books they can read. These students miss the fun of reading books that their peers enjoy.

Scholastic offers a product called WiggleWorks, which allows teachers to change the onscreen background and text color to make text more accessible for children to read. This software will also read individual words or pages to the children, allowing those with varied abilities to enjoy the stories (Rose, 2013). The Thinking Reader software and other online programs allow children to access grade-level text. The children can experience the same book as their peers and join class discussions.

- **E-books:** Digital book options have made it possible for children to be exposed to a variety of literature, regardless of their reading level. Research shows that children are far more confident, contribute more to class discussions, and read more when they can use digital technology to aid with reading (O'Neill and Dalton, 2002). A textbook with additional visuals or organization features built into the original design supports students with processing difficulties by helping them organize their reading. They do not stand out as special education adaptations and are not limited to students with a disability. All students benefit from additional visuals and organizers.

Increasingly, interactive digital books are available on all subjects for all ages. For example, preschool children can listen on a tablet to a digital story about the letter *M*, touch the *M*, and hear the sound. On another page, they can match the pictures with the same sound. The interactive book provides engagement and skills practice in a way that is not available in a paper book.

> One of my students, eight-year-old Sarai, was reading well below grade level. Still, when it came time to pick out a library book for her independent reading time, she would pick the biggest book she could find even though she could not read it. She would show her friends the book she was reading and sit and pretend to read. She was embarrassed by her low level and did not want the other children to see her with an easy book.
>
> After writing a successful grant for e-book readers, I was able to offer e-books as an option for any child who was interested. The e-readers opened a whole new world of reading for all students. Sarai was excited to pick books she could read and enjoy on the e-reader without fear of being embarrassed by her reading level. She started reading more, not only during selected reading time but also just for fun.

Several years later, she wrote me a letter explaining the impact on her when she was younger. Now she is a successful reader and student. The e-readers were popular with all the students. So simple, yet so powerful.

The expectations are still high, but how children meet a goal can vary. Children will soar when they have multiple ways to learn and show what they know. In a first-grade classroom, a teacher uses UDL during drop everything and read (DEAR) time. A child in a wheelchair uses a switch to activate the computer to read a story. Other children listen to stories on an iPad. Some are reading independently, while others use software with books at various grade levels to read or hear. A child who is blind is reading using Braille. Allowing each student to read with appropriate accommodations allows this teacher to utilize universal design. All the children benefit from being included in this activity (O'Neill, 2000).

Math and Science

Picture a classroom in which all students gain math and science skills with access to the accommodations they need to succeed. Some children are engrossed in science experiments, while others were engaged in math explorations. The student-led education with high expectations and a rigorous curriculum allows the children to highlight their skills in multiple ways. They write, discuss, make predictions, and document their progress. Children explore and learn while their teachers guide them. Documentation and data with pictures and writing are displayed in the classroom at child level, so the children can revisit what they have learned throughout the school year. The teachers also collaborate regularly to use their skills to build a solid team to support the children.

When teaching math and science, educators can set the stage for highly engaged classrooms with the UDL mindset, providing easily accessible accommodations and assistive technology to anyone needing additional support and scaffolding to allow children with a variety of abilities to achieve. Start with one lesson or one change to the environment and build on those skills because every change, whether large or small, will support children's learning.

Many factors affect children's success in math. Muscle strength and fine-motor skills affect a child's ability to write numbers or to use manipulatives. Some children struggle with one-to-one correspondence, leading to problems with counting. Poor reading skills affect children's ability to understand story problems. Behavior challenges and focus issues undermine learning.

For children who have a hard time with one-to-one correspondence, math manipulatives allow them to feel and see while learning. Visualization of concepts can also be supported by graphic organizers, such as tens charts, hundreds charts, place-value charts, graph paper, and graphs.

Calculators can be useful learning tools that don't replace learning math facts but allow a child to have fun checking their answers. There are also talking calculators that say the numbers when you touch them. Handheld early childhood math tools and toys offer a variety of interactive math learning games that keep students engaged while teaching them important concepts. Wipe-off boards work well during math so everyone can participate in a class math activity.

In early childhood classrooms, children can develop their understanding of math concepts through children's books, songs, and rhyme, as well as in play-based learning and explorations. Educators can model how to play with math in the center area, asking questions such as, "How many connect rings long is your block tower?" and "How many counters can you put in the container?" Children can grow their math skills in a safe and supportive classroom that encourages math exploration and learning. Everyone is learning and exploring math at their level and gaining a greater understanding of math concepts (McLennan, 2014).

Because children enjoy and learn through exploration and experimentation, they will naturally gravitate toward science tools and materials. Science tools can include magnifying glasses, goggles, sorting items, microscopes, large tweezers, rulers, measuring cups, spoons, scales, test tubes, bug viewers, and magnets. Items to explore can include rocks, shells, leaves, seeds, sand, water, plants, and animals. Children can record their findings in science journals and learn more through science books on their topics of interest. Science works well for all ability levels, and few accommodations are needed for young children.

In my kindergarten classroom, the children learned about our solar system and space. In art, they used books with pictures of planets to choose a planet to make from salt dough and paint. On the science tables, I placed a variety of rocks along with magnifying glasses, paper, writing utensils, and clipboards with which to make pictures of their discoveries. In the computer area, a microscope connected to the computer and allowed the children to view slides of the planets that also showed up on the computer screen. They made slideshows with planets in the computer lab since they had already learned to make slides during the school year. In the writing area, I provided pictures with words and sentence starters for students to use to write science words, make a sentence using the sentence starters, and create an image to go with their words or sentences. In math, they made patterns with images of asteroids and planets. That year, students had one day a week when a family member could join us after lunch to read books. Many family members read books on space and the planets to the children. The children even set up a pretend science museum and displayed the planets they had made in art. They were busy learning and exploring during the entire unit. By seeing and hearing the information in different ways and formats, the class was able to learn and be successful in their scientific understanding.

● ● ●

Lesson planning with UDL works well from early childhood and beyond. It starts with a SMART goal while considering the multiple paths children could choose to meet the goal. As educators switch to implementing the UDL guidelines, it is essential to understand that the average child is a myth. Instead of planning for "average," plan for the outer limits. Look for potential barriers and find ways to help children navigate around them. Use low-, medium-, or high-tech and allow multiple ways for students to show what they know. Strategically plan ways to engage, encourage, and challenge the children to become expert learners.

It is okay to start small and not try to do it all. The critical point is to make education more equitable and accessible. Use the cycle of planning, teaching, assessing, tracking data, reflecting, and adjusting lessons as you incorporate UDL into planning and instruction. Once you see your entire class of children engaged, exploring, and discovering, it will be impossible to return to teaching using traditional methods.

Schools can no longer ignore the potential benefits of universal design for learning. Now is the time to start a UDL movement in education. It provides students with the tools and curriculum to make education accessible for all. Brain research advances have helped researchers develop innovative ways to help students become expert learners. As Miss Frizzle of the Magic School Bus series says, "Take chances, make mistakes, and get messy!" Don't be afraid to make mistakes and get messy while navigating changes in the classroom that will help and support children. Students thrive when given the tools to be successful.

Appendix A: Low-, Medium-, and High-Tech Tools

Low-Tech Tools

Low-tech tools are readily available items that usually do not require extra training but make learning more accessible to children. Teachers can use them in a variety of learning activities.

LANGUAGE ARTS AND MATH

Low-tech tools are great for supporting fine-motor development and literacy skills. For example, offer several types of paper, such as the following:

- **Paper with raised lines:** Raised lines help children who need tactile input when forming letters, numbers, or words.

- **Paper with color-coded lines:** Color-coded lines help with readability.

- **Paper in a variety of colors:** Some children can see better when the paper is colored rather than white, which can have glare. If a child struggles with letters, numbers, or words on paper or in a book, trying colored paper may help.

You can also use Wikki Stix, thin waxy sticks that add texture and can stick to any paper, which makes the activity multisensory for children who learn better with tactile input.

Different types of writing and coloring utensils can make it easier for children to complete fine-motor activities such as writing or coloring:

- Little chubby animal markers are great for three- and four-year-olds who struggle to grasp thin markers or crayons.

- Adaptive writing utensils are readily available at most office stores. They can help children with weak hand muscles, poor fine-motor skills, or mobility issues to grip the writing utensil or write with greater ease. Some children with weak hand muscles lack the strength or fine-motor skills to hold a traditional writing utensil. Other writing utensils put less stress on a child's hand, which for a child with weak hand muscles, can make the difference in whether they endure hand pain while writing or not. There are writing utensils that are wider for small hands and some in a "y" shape, making writing or drawing easier.

- Educators can buy various tools relatively inexpensively and try them out to see what works best for their students. It is easy for adults to think a child is being fussy for no reason when they complain that their hands hurt while writing, but for some children, this is true, and they should be allowed alternatives when writing or drawing that are more accessible and fun for them.

- Various pencil grips have the benefit of helping with hand placement on the pencil, providing comfort for the child, making writing fun, and helping with weak hand muscles and poor fine-motor skills. I usually purchase a variety of different colors and kinds.

- Foam grips can help children who struggle to turn pages in a book. To create a foam grip, glue a piece of foam on a large popsicle stick or clothespin, and attach it to fine-motor tasks to make them more accessible. One way to attach the clothespin, foam grip, or popsicle stick is to use Velcro on the book pages and the item. Put soft Velcro on the book's pages, so it can also be used without the adaptation. The adapted book will allow a child who struggles with fine-motor skills to turn the pages independently.

- Slant boards work well for children struggling with handwriting or who have poor muscle tone in their hands. I offer instructions for making a slanted desk on page 128.

- Sticky notes have a variety of uses. They work well for color-coding folders, books, and supplies. You can offer them to children who are beginning to form letters and numbers when they make a mistake. A sticky note can quickly cover the letter or number so the child can try again without having to erase or be upset that what they wrote isn't correct.

- Highlighters come in large sizes for little hands and smaller sizes for older children. Preschool children can highlight all the same letters, shapes, or numbers on a page. In beginning phonics games, children can mark their answers. Children in kindergarten through second grade can use highlighters to mark or trace letters, numbers, and words or to highlight text with teacher modeling. Some highlighters make only a dot, which is fun for children who are learning number sense; they can make the number of dots that a numeral represents. The teacher can also use highlighters to highlight lines on paper for a child with visual issues to make the lines stand out.

- Bookmarks are useful for highlighting one row at a time, making it easier for beginning readers to find their place. This is especially helpful for children who have difficulty tracking text.

- Color overlays are transparent plastic sheets that can easily be placed over any print for a child. They are great to help with glare from fluorescent lighting, which, for light-sensitive children, can make reading difficult.

- Different font sizes can make it easier for children to see. At young ages, they haven't all had their eyes tested. For some, small print is not only hard to see but hard for their eyes to track. A font does not have to be giant, but if one size is too small, experiment and see what size works. Larger font sizes also can make reading easier for children who have dyslexia.

- Graphic organizers help to organize what the child is working on visually; although not used as much in preschool, children in kindergarten through second grade use them often. A graphic organizer can be straightforward with pictures that children are sorting into categories. For beginning writers, it could be a story web with images or words, or comparing characters or settings in pictures or words, or organizing beginning stories with visual support.

- Math manipulatives are great for learning math skills, from sorting shapes to working with tens and ones.

- Virtual math manipulatives allow children to move them on a tablet, computer, or smartboard.

SENSORY AND OTHER CHALLENGES

- Noise-canceling headphones block classroom sounds and help a child from becoming overwhelmed. For some children with sensory sensitivity, noise can hurt their ears. Even children without sensory issues may prefer wearing them because they do not like noise.

- Fidgets are small items a child can hold to help them focus. I keep a fidget tub with various textures and shapes in the sensory area. Children can use them as they work on projects or listen to a story at circle time.

- Weighted items, such as lap pads and stuffed animals, help children feel calmer and more focused. I keep a classroom set so anyone can use them anytime. They are great for circle time, at the tables, or during any activity when the child is sitting.

- Various seating options can help children with focus while they work or participate in circle time.

- Step stools can help a child who is too small for the chairs available to be more comfortable.

- A quiet area with a small table and chair or beanbag chair can help children who feel overwhelmed or who simply want to do an activity on their own.

BEHAVIOR INCENTIVE CHARTS

A first/then chart works well for children who are struggling to follow directions or complete an activity. On the chart, the teacher can Velcro a picture of what is expected first and then a picture of what the child can do next. For example, a picture of circle time under the word *first*

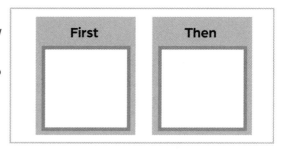

tells the child that circle time happens first. A picture of a preferred item, task, or edible under the word *then* lets the child know that participating in circle time will be followed by the preferred item, task, or edible. This works well for children who are unable to use a token chart and delay their reward.

An "I am working for . . ." token chart motivates children to be cooperative and follow directions. Create a chart that has a place to Velcro a picture of something a child is working for, and add four or five spots below the goal picture where you can attach stars. I use token charts to motivate children to complete tasks or follow directions. I start by building excitement with the token chart and give the child a menu

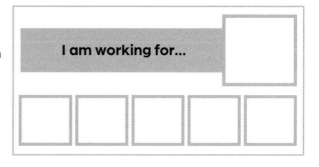

of choices to work toward. One child loved Thomas the Tank Engine, so I had a small bucket of train cars that he could work toward. When he completed a task, I would put a token on his chart. When the chart was filled, I would set a timer and give him the train cars to play with.

Using token charts is often all the motivation that some children need to complete tasks or follow directions. If a student is struggling, I award the tokens faster at first, then I slowly lengthen the time between earning tokens. The idea is to wean them off the token charts eventually, but if done too quickly, you may have to start over again with frequent tokens. I have had children who needed a token every few minutes, and I have had students who could go through an entire activity between earning tokens. The key is to be positive and not make it an adverse event. For example, I would not say, "You will not earn tokens if you do not get to work." Instead, if a child made any move toward compliance, I would say, "Wow! I can tell you are starting to work. You are almost earning your first token. I am so proud of you." Educators must be careful of how they verbalize behavior motivation to keep it positive for children.

I also keep multiple menu items so that the student can decide each time what they are working for at that moment. Children change, and what motivates them today might not motivate them tomorrow. The menu choices will depend on the child's age. Choices could be playdough, puzzles, time with friends, quiet reading time, taking off their shoes, or time on a tablet or computer. For students with significant behavior challenges, teachers have to get creative. I sometimes use a student's specific interests. One student asked for the FBI warning shown at the beginning of videos. He would work to see that screen for a couple of minutes. Having a child off task with a preferred item for a few minutes is better than losing the entire day to noncompliant behavior.

Interestingly, it doesn't bother other children when one or more students have token charts. There are times that I have used them with an entire group, but it is a huge challenge and is optional for this method to be successful.

- Visual schedules promote independence and decrease stress for children because they can refer to them to know what is next. They can be posted for the entire class to use or can be individually set up for each child, allowing them to work independently throughout their day by checking their schedule when prompted to move to another activity.

- Visual steps help children follow multistep directions and build independence. For example, if there is a specific sequence as a child arrives, the visual steps should be posted in that area. For preschool children, it might include:

  1. A picture of a backpack to remind the children to hang up their backpacks.
  2. A picture of a coat to remind the children to hang up their coats.
  3. A picture of the location they need to go to next.

- For kindergarteners through second-graders, the list with visuals might be posted on the board and include:

  1. Hang up backpack.
  2. Put away lunch.
  3. Sit at the table.
  4. Look at books.

- Visual steps can be posted for handwashing, using the bathroom, playing a game, or participating in circle time. Encourage parents to add visuals at home to support children who would benefit. Similar to visual steps, visual strips in learning centers help children to know what to do with the materials. They are helpful for all children.

Medium-Tech Tools

A number of medium-tech tools support not only fine-motor skills but also literacy skills.

- Adapted books are children's books in which the teacher puts additional visuals to support children's understanding. Additional visuals are helpful even if the book has pictures on every page because they make the books interactive and engaging. Teachers can use felt or laminated card stock for the pictures. One way to use them is to place additional pictures that would be helpful on each page. Another way is to place the images as the teacher or child reads the story. For example, as a child reads *The Three Little Pigs*, he could move the pigs around as the story progresses.

- Digital audiobooks are great for all children for building language skills, beginning reading skills, and comprehension. They also allow children who are behind their peers in reading to listen to the same popular books in their classroom. Public libraries typically offer a wealth of children's books, and some libraries have early childhood interactive learning games too. Epic! (https://www.getepic.com) is free for teachers and has a comprehensive book section for toddlers and up.

- E-book readers are a great assistive technology tool. Children of all ages can learn to use them. These tools allow for adjusting font size and background color, and they are often cheaper than tablets. Children find them remarkably motivating and can use them for picture books or beginning readers. They also work well for children who are behind their peers and do not want to be embarrassed by reading easy books. No one can tell if a child is reading a two-hundred-page book or a ten-page book when it's loaded on the e-reader.

- Speech-to-text and text-to-speech accommodations in tablets and computers allow children to write a sentence or story by simply clicking on a mic and talking. They then click on the correct icon to have it read back to them. I have used this with kindergarteners and older children. It is highly motivating, and each year the technology gets better. (Keep in mind that it does not work well for a child who has significant articulation errors when talking.) Speech-to-text also works for answering short questions using software such as Google Forms, which can have text and pictures inserted by the teacher.

MATH SKILLS

Calculators or child-friendly handheld math toys are available to help with math skills. They can also serve as motivating tools because anything electronic is popular with all children. Some calculators have large buttons and additional visuals with limited choices. It is tricky to know whether a child should use a calculator. As educators, we want children to learn the basic skills first. Still, for some children, learning how to use a calculator is a life skill because they cannot learn basic calculating skills.

SENSORY CHALLENGES

A single-student quiet area can help children who are easily distracted or have sensory issues and prefer to work in a calm place. It is also helpful for any child who wants to be away from the group for a little bit to recharge and relax. I have used quiet areas with kindergarteners through third graders; they are favorite spots for all my students. If you make the area a privilege and make a big deal that it can only be used if the child is well-behaved, the entire class will want to use the quiet space. If you treat it as a time-out, no one will want to use it.

High-Tech Tools

- The Google Education Suite—Docs, Sheets, Slides, Forms, and Microsoft Office—can give children engaging ways to write and read. When I taught kindergarten, they learned how to make slides for a topic we were studying. We started small with working on typing in their names, then they learned how to type a sentence with sentence stems. As the year went on, they became more proficient and began learning beginning technology, language, vocabulary, phonics, and reading skills. They also learned how to cooperate and teach each other skills they learned. It was fun to see a child go ahead of what I had taught, get excited, and then show his peers. The first child who realized they could animate pictures and text was very popular in the kindergarten classroom. His self-esteem made a considerable jump. When I used the PowerPoint lesson in a first-grade classroom, one of my students with significant learning disabilities was the best in the class on the computer.

- Reading A–Z is a site with beginning phonics, phonological awareness, stories, graphic organizers, vocabulary, and more.

- PebbleGo is a children's visual encyclopedia that reads every word and has many pictures.

- Virtual Field Trips (https://virtualfieldtrips.org/video-library) lets you take children on virtual trips to farms, zoos, museums, state parks, Mars, and more.

- Google Earth will also let you and the children visit places worldwide.

- ClassDojo is a free, motivating, behavior-incentive app. Each child can pick a different avatar, and the teacher can give points to the whole group or to individual children. It makes a noise when they get a point, so my young students were motivated.

- GoNoodle is a website that has many ways for children to be active and have fun with mini brain breaks. Children are more engaged in lessons when they have breaks.

- Seesaw is an online program allowing teachers to create lessons or use lessons already made and share them with their students in person or virtually. The free version limits teachers to a certain number of lessons, but many school districts have subscriptions. During the COVID-19 pandemic, this worked well even with my nonverbal students with autism. Young children may need parental support with virtual lessons. I have also used Seesaw on the smartboard with my students. They like that they can color, write, or take pictures while learning. Teachers can add audio or video directions for the children to hear, so reading is unnecessary. This can be a way to individualize instruction and give a child an assignment on a tablet or computer.

- Starfall offers activities on letters, numbers, colors, songs, beginning stories, and rhymes at various early childhood levels. Some areas are free, and other areas are subscription-based.

- ABC Mouse is a subscription learning site for young children. It offers learning games, activities, and songs.

- A classroom FM system amplifies the teacher's voice, so that children are better able to tune into what she is saying. The teacher wears a microphone that uses radio waves to transfer to the speakers in the classroom. This is especially good for children with hearing issues, auditory processing disorder, ADHD, or ASD.

- Robots can go to school for children who are sick and cannot attend in person. A robot is physically in the classroom and transmits audio and video to the child on a tablet. A pilot program in Madison, Wisconsin, allowed a child in the hospital to talk with peers using an iPad. She could move the robot to circle time to see a story with the rest of the class. She worked on the same projects as her peers. Excellent teacher planning allowed her to have all the same materials at the hospital to do whatever her peers do. This is a fantastic way to connect children who would otherwise be isolated (Glaser, 2022).

- Wearable artificial intelligence (AI) or wearable tech can be worn like a watch and receive alerts about when the device detects changes that could indicate the need to calm down or other signs to help the child self-monitor their behavior.

- The OCR Instantly Pro app lets a teacher take a photo from a hardcopy document and convert it into a text format that then is converted to speech. Some other apps and programs can also perform this task.

- A smartboard looks like a large-screen television with a touch screen. It allows teachers to project anything from their computer onto the screen. Various smartboard software and interactive learning games that are highly engaging can also be used during instruction. There are also smartboard tables for early childhood with learning games to engage young children.

- A document camera connects to a computer and can display on the computer monitor or a smartboard. Teachers can share anything they want to project on the screen for everyone to see, such as a science experiment, a book the teacher is reading aloud, or an activity the teacher wants to do with the children.

DEVICES FOR CHILDREN WHO NEED ADDITIONAL SUPPORT

- Augmentative and alternative communication (AAC) devices or apps allow children with significant language delays to communicate. AACs can also be used instead of a picture communication book.

- Artificial intelligence (AI) wearable devices can help people on the autism spectrum. These devices include apps, special glasses, and smart watches. Studies show that they help improve social skills (Voss et al., 2019).

Appendix B:
Do-It-Yourself (DIY) Educational Materials

DIY QUIET OR STUDY AREA

The DIY quiet area is made from PVC pipes and can be constructed to fit around a desk or table.

The number of PVC pipes depends on the size needed for the project.

Materials

4 T-socket connectors

8 corner connectors

PVC pipes

Fabric or plastic shower curtain

Saw

Measuring tape

How to Make It

1. It is best to measure and draw a plan of what works for the size needed. Measure the width, length, and height of the desk or table you are working with.

2. Cut the lengths of PVC pipe 4 inches longer than your measurements.

3. For the back of the study area, slide two T-socket connectors onto each of the vertical pipes.

4. Connect the top crosspiece to the vertical pipes using two corner connectors.

5. Connect the bottom crosspiece into the lower T-socket connectors.

6. Insert the bottom of each vertical pipe into a corner connector.

7. For the sides of the study area, insert a PVC pipe into a lower corner connector at the bottom of the vertical pipes.

8. Insert PVC pipes into the upper T-socket connectors.

9. Slide corner connectors onto the ends of the remaining exposed ends of the PVC pipes.

10. Insert two vertical pipes into the corner connectors at the top and bottom.

11. The sides can be covered in a variety of ways. You can sew fabric to make little curtains, and the PVC pipes can go through the top of the fabric like curtain rods. Alternatively, you can drape material over each side of the enclosure. You can cut a shower curtain to fit the sides and secure the pieces with duct tape.

12. Position the quiet area around the desk or table.

How to Use It

Explain to the children that this is an area anyone can use when they need a little quiet time to help them concentrate. If you make it unique, then all the children will enjoy using it. Avoid introducing it as a time-out area; no one will want to use it if you do.

DIY Sensory Materials

Weighted items can be calming for children and adults. Before using a weighted item with a child, consult the school occupational therapist for the recommended best practices for the age group you teach. Using a weighted item on a child all day is not recommended.

WEIGHTED BLANKET

This is a project for someone who is experienced with sewing.

Materials

2 large pieces of fabric, bedsheets, or blankets in the size needed

Thread, scissors, pins, and basic sewing supplies

Sewing machine

Weighted pellets

Funnel

Velcro

How to Make It

Method 1:

1. Put the two pieces of fabric, two sheets, or two blankets together face to face, matching the corners.

2. Sew three sides of the fabric. Leave one side open.

3. Sew vertical rows into the fabric to create channels to hold the weighted beads.

4. Fill the channels with weighted beads.

5. Sew the remaining side shut.

Method 2:

1. Cut fabric into 4" x 4" (or larger) squares. Sew the fabric squares onto a blanket to create pockets. Remember to leave one side of each pocket open.

2. Sew or adhere Velcro onto the inside edge of each pocket opening to create a closure. This will make it possible to pull the beanbags out before washing.

3. Cut fabric into squares one inch smaller than the pockets. You will need double the number of pockets you have made. So, if you made ten pockets, you will need twenty fabric squares.

4. Put two pieces together, and sew them on three sides. Fill them with weighted pellets to make beanbags. Sew them shut.

5. Slide the beanbags into the pockets, and close the pockets with the Velcro closures.

How to Use It

A weighted blanket is calming for a child, especially for a child with ADHD or autism spectrum disorder. It can be challenging to wash, unless you make it with pockets so that you can remove the weights.

These can be calming for all children, especially those with ADHD or autism spectrum disorder. My mother made a class set for me, which I kept in a tub in the classroom that my students could access at any time.

Materials

Sensory-friendly fabric, such as cotton or fleece

Weighted beads

Funnel

Scissors, pins, and basic sewing supplies

Sewing machine

Measuring tape

How to Make It

1. Measure the fabric and cut two 14" x 20" pieces.

2. Fold over the edges of each fabric piece and pin them in place. A 1" margin works well. Sew around the edges of both fabric pieces. Place the two fabric pieces together with the wrong sides out.

3. Sew them together around three sides, leaving one end open.

4. Turn the fabric right-side out.

5. Sew three rows across the fabric to create channels to hold the weighted beads.

6. Consult the school occupational therapist to determine the appropriate weight for the age group you teach. Measure that amount of weighted beads, and then divide the beads into four groups.

7. Fill each channel.

8. Sew the seam shut.

9. Optional: Make a cover or use a pillowcase for the lap pad, which you can easily remove for washing.

How to Use It

Like any school supply, a weighted lap pad comes with rules and responsibilities children must follow to have the privilege to use one. Using a weighted item on a child all day is not recommended.

WEIGHTED STUFFED ANIMAL

Weighted stuffed animals are a great sensory idea to use during circle time to help keep students calm while they listen to stories and sing songs.

Materials

Any stuffed animal

Weighted pellets

Funnel

Needle, thread, and scissors

How to Make It

1. Carefully open a 2- to 4-inch seam in the stuffed animal.

2. Add weighted pellets

3. Sew the seam shut.

How to Use It

The stuffed animals are washable. If each child has an assigned stuffed animal, it keeps the spread of germs to a minimum.

SENSORY TUB IDEAS

I use plastic tubs with lids that are easy to store and pull out as needed. All sorts of materials will work as your base material, such as the following:

aquarium rocks	cotton balls or pompoms
large beads	cloud dough* or playdough
birdseed (without capsaicin added)	craft feathers
blocks or LEGO bricks	cut-up straws (for children over three years)
bubble wrap	
cardboard tubes or small boxes	cut-up pool noodles
	fabric strips, ribbon

* You can find simple recipes on the internet for cloud dough.

fake snow	pine cones
foam pieces	play sand
foil	puzzle pieces
gift-wrapping paper or tissue paper	seashells
	sponges
ice	sticks
Kidfetti	water
kinetic sand	water beads
magazines, scrap paper, or shredded paper	yarn
packing peanuts	

Next, add any theme or learning suggestions, such as the following, to your tub.

- **Literacy:**

  - Add letters and words, which can be plastic or made with card stock and laminated.

  - Put laminated card stock letters or words into the tub along with plastic letters or playdough for children to form the letters or words.

  - Add objects that start with specific letters or sounds and let children practice matching them. Laminated words can be used the same way.

  - Storybooks can also be part of the sensory-tub theme. Pick a book and make the tub around the theme of the book. For children who are writing, follow up by encouraging them to write a sentence or story about the tub theme. It is highly motivating when they have a multisensory approach to writing.

  - Place laminated letters or words into the tub for children to trace in sensory material such as different kinds of sand, beads, and so on.

- **Math:**

  - Use plastic or laminated card stock for numbers, math facts, number lines, tens and ones chart, bar graphs, and more.

- Add number cards and objects or playdough and let the children make sets to match the numbers. Add math facts with equation cards and manipulatives (which can be any small item they can count), number charts, or number lines to let children practice solving equations.

- Practice measurement and volume by adding measuring cups and spoons with water, sand, or other sensory materials that students can have fun exploring and using fine-motor skills filling measuring cups and pouring into other containers.

- Practice length and height by adding plastic rulers and small measuring tapes with a variety of objects to measure.

- Provide pattern cards and items that can be made into patterns. These items could be of different colors and sizes or in shapes that can be repeated to make a pattern.

- Practice tens and ones by adding number cards and a tens/ones chart with base-ten blocks to explore and build the numbers.

- **Science:**

  A sensory tub can follow the theme of a story read during circle time. For example, the teacher might read a book about digging for dinosaurs, then add items to create an archeologist tub.

  - **Archeology:** Bury plastic dinosaurs or make plaster bones for children to discover in cloud dough or different types of sand. Give them paintbrushes to uncover the little dinosaurs and "fossils." They can also have clipboards with paper to draw their discoveries.

  - **Beach/Ocean:** In water or shredded blue paper, put plastic fish, seashells, seals, otters, turtles, whales, octopus, starfish, toy boats, and rocks. To make a pretend beach, set a container filled with any type of sand and plastic people inside the larger tub.

  - **Farm:** Add plastic farm animals, fences, people, toy tractors, and other farm equipment.

  - **Forest:** Add pine cones, rocks, plastic forest animals, plastic trees, plastic or real leaves

- **Insects and bugs:** Add plastic insects, spiders, and other "bugs."

- **Magnets:** Add magnets and items that children can test to see if the magnets will pick them up.

- **Medical/Health:** Fill a bin with cotton balls, and add toy doctor kits and either dolls or stuffed animals for children to give checkups.

- **Sink or float:** Fill a bin with water, and add items that children can test to see if they sink or float.

- **Space:** Add planets, stars, rockets, astronauts, sand, and rocks. The planets can be plastic, Styrofoam, different-size pompoms, or baked dough in the shapes of the planets.

- **Penguins:** Add fake snow or ice and toy penguins. You can make an "iceberg" by freezing water in a gallon milk jug and cutting the jug away. Children love this!

- **Pond:** Add plastic frogs, leaves, sticks, and rocks to water.

- **Rain forest:** Add trees, plastic animals including snakes, sloths, and frogs, and spray bottles with water to make rain.

- **Desert:** Add plastic animals and plastic cacti to sand.

- **Seasons:**

  - **Winter:** ice and/or fake snow, plastic shovels, plastic people, penguins, laminated card stock sleds, and transportation vehicles

  - **Spring:** birdseed or shredded brown paper, toy gardening tools, magnifying glasses, and plastic insects

  - **Summer:** sand or water and toy animals or boats

  - **Fall:** leaves, sticks, mulch, rocks, gourds that look like pumpkins and other shapes, fall color pompoms, and beads

- **Art:**

  Set up different bins with types of art media for children to explore.

  - Fingerpaint, painting tools, and paper

  - Playdough or modeling clay

  - Beads, ribbon, fabric scraps, wallpaper scraps, construction paper, and glue

  - Nature items such as sticks, leaves, and small rocks, along with paint and paper or playdough

RECIPE FOR COOKED PLAYDOUGH

This playdough is soft and lasts a long time if kept in an airtight container.

Materials

2 cups all-purpose flour	measuring cups and spoons
3/4 cup salt	pot
4 teaspoons cream of tartar	stove
2 cups lukewarm water	spoon
2 tablespoons vegetable oil	cutting board or rolling mat
food coloring	plastic gloves (optional)

How to Make It

1. In a pot over medium heat, mix the flour and next four ingredients until all the moisture is removed and the dough is almost impossible to stir. If there is too much water left, the playdough will be gooey. If you plan to use only one color, the food coloring can be added during cooking. Lay the dough on the counter and let it cool until it is safe to touch.

2. Knead the dough for a few minutes. (Wear gloves to keep food coloring from staining your skin.)

3. Divide the playdough and add food coloring to each ball you make.

4. Let the playdough cool completely, and then put it into an airtight container.

DIY SUPERHERO "SUPER STUDENT" CAPE

Students love to be recognized and to have a special day.

Materials

Fabric, such as remnants

Scissors

Measuring tape

Bias tape 1/2" wide

Basic sewing supplies, thread

Sewing machine

Iron

Iron-on letters

How to Make It

1. Cut a piece of fabric. The size will vary depending on the age of the child. Measure the length and adjust so the cape is 4–6 inches off the ground. The width should be twice as wide as you need, so when you gather it, it will be wide enough.

2. Sew a quarter-inch seam all around the edge of the material and then sew around again, so all the rough edges are tucked under. Alternatively, you can fold the fabric one-quarter inch and iron it. Then, fold the fabric another quarter inch and iron again, and then sew around the edge.

3. Using a sewing machine, sew two rows of basting stiches parallel across the top side of the fabric. Then, pull the strings to gather the material.

4. Sew the bias tape across the top, leaving enough on both sides to tie the cape in the front.

5. Use iron-on letters to add "Super Student" to the back of the cape.

How to Use It

Safety note: I don't let them wear the capes to PE or outside.

I use the superhero cape for the student of the day or for children to earn to wear during specific subjects during the day.

DIY SLANTED DESK

Slanted desks are helpful for students when they write. Purchased desks can be expensive, but this DIY version is easy to make.

Materials

3-inch three-ring binder

One clipboard

Velcro

How to Make It

Use Velcro to attach the clipboard to one side of the binder. Place the Velcro to allow the binder to connect both horizontally and vertically, allowing students to have flexibility when writing.

How to Use It

Students can clip their paper onto the clipboard and work without having their paper slip off.

DIY COMMUNICATION BOOK

A picture communication book is helpful for children who are nonverbal or have few verbal skills to learn that communication is a way to obtain what they need or get help. Using the book reduces frustration and challenging behavior.

Materials

Plastic binder that can easily be cut

Velcro

Scissors

Photos or clip art of classroom materials and common actions

Card stock or index cards

Laminator or clear contact paper

Sturdy plastic divider pages

Three-hole punch

How to Make It

1. Place the binder on a table, with the opening on the right.

2. Cut off 3 inches from the top cover on the right side of the binder.

3. Trim off half an inch around the strip that was cut off.

4. Put Velcro across the entire strip, soft half on top and rough half on the bottom.

5. Put another piece of soft Velcro on the binder side that was not cut. This will allow the cut piece to be taken off and on for communication.

6. Put the sturdy divider pages into the binder. I trim the pages so they do not hang out and then punch new holes using a three-hole punch.

7. Put soft Velcro in rows of three or four across the pages and on the top of the side of the binder.

8. Cut out clip art or trim photos to fit onto card stock or index cards.

9. Laminate or cover the cards with clear contact paper. Put the rough sides of Velcro onto the backs of the cards.

How to Use It

Add a few pictures at a time while training the student in how to use the binder to communicate. Add more images as the child is ready. I used to teach my students by putting pictures of preferred items and letting them have an item only if they requested it using the communication book.

Appendix C: Forms, Charts, and Visuals

This chart represents the UDL Guidelines. Learn more at https://www.cast.org/

Provide multiple means of **Engagement**	Provide multiple means of **Representation**	Provide multiple means of **Action & Expression**
Affective Networks The "WHY" of Learning	Recognition Networks The "WHAT" of Learning	Strategic Networks The "HOW" of Learning
Access		
Provide options for **Recruiting Interest** (7) • Optimize individual choice and autonomy (7.1) • Optimize relevance, value, and authenticity (7.2) • Minimize threats and distractions (7.3)	Provide options for **Perception** (1) • Offer ways of customizing the display of information (1.1) • Offer alternatives for auditory information (1.2) • Offer alternatives for visual information (1.3)	Provide options for **Physical Action** (4) • Vary the methods for response and navigation (4.1) • Optimize access to tools and assistive technologies (4.2)
Build		
Provide options for **Sustaining Effort & Persistence** (8) • Heighten salience of goals and objectives (8.1) • Vary demands and resources to optimize challenge (8.2) • Foster collaboration and community (8.3) • Increase mastery-oriented feedback (8.4)	Provide options for **Language & Symbols** (2) • Clarify vocabulary and symbols (2.1) • Clarify syntax and structure (2.2) • Support decoding of text, mathematical notation, and symbols (2.3) • Promote understanding across languages (2.4) • Illustrate through multiple media (2.5)	Provide options for **Expression & Communication** (5) • Use multiple media for communication (5.1) • Use multiple tools for construction and composition (5.2) • Build fluencies with graduated levels of support for practice and performance (5.3)
Internalize		
Provide options for **Self Regulation** (9) • Promote expectations and beliefs that optimize motivation (9.1) • Facilitate personal coping skills and strategies (9.2) • Develop self-assessment and reflection (9.3)	Provide options for **Comprehension** (3) • Activate or supply background knowledge (3.1) • Highlight patterns, critical features, big ideas, and relationships (3.2) • Guide information processing and visualization (3.3) • Maximize transfer and generalization (3.4)	Provide options for **Executive Functions** (6) • Guide appropriate goal-setting (6.1) • Support planning and strategy development (6.2) • Facilitate managing information and resources (6.3) • Enhance capacity for monitoring progress (6.4)
Goal		
Expert learners who are...		
Purposeful & Motivated	Resourceful & Knowledgeable	Strategic & Goal-Directed

CAST. 2018a. Universal Design for Learning Guidelines. Version 2.2. Wakefield, MA: CAST. http://udlguidelines.cast.org

Forms to Track Data

Like a typical lesson, a UDL lesson encourages collecting data to track progress and adjust future lessons as needed. One method is using Google Forms to create a form where the educator can quickly take data. Then, the form can be opened in Google Sheets and converted into charts and graphs.

QR codes can be made for each form to make it easy to scan, open the form, and take data. The free site that I currently use is https://www.the-qrcode-generator.com/

MATH GOAL: RECOGNITION 1–10

Child's name: _____

Date: _____

How many numbers out of 1–10 did the child say correctly?

1	2	3	4	5	6	7	8	9	10
O	O	O	O	O	O	O	O	O	O

I have a form for every goal for my students. I also use the forms to track behavior and parent contacts.

Sample Visuals

TOKEN CHART

A child who needs extra encouragement to keep working but can delay the reward can use a token chart. Put Velcro on the different areas, laminate stars or any small picture that could be motivating for the tokens, and use either an image or words to put in the reward.

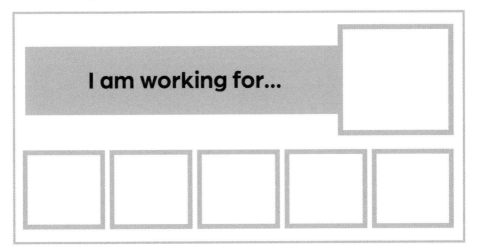

Children who need extra encouragement to keep working can use a First/Then chart. Use pictures or words under each heading. For example, First Work, Then Puzzle. It is highly motivating for any age.

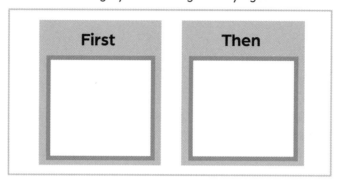

ADDING VISUALS TO A BOOK

Any book can be adapted to add picture support for children who need visuals to be successful.

Materials

Clip art or photos relevant to words in book

Laminator or clear contact paper

Velcro dots

How to Make It

1. Print or take photos to clearly represent the words the child is learning.

2. Cut them out and laminate the pictures or cover them with clear contact paper.

3. Add Velcro dots to the backs of the images and to the pages where the words appear.

How to Use It

Adaptive books help with building language and communication skills and comprehension skills. The educator can use the adapted books to increase student motivation and engagement while reading the story. Also, students can use the interactive, adaptive books in the book center. They quickly become the favorite books of the students.

Appendix D:
Books for Educators on Learning Variabilities

ADD and ADHD

Barkley, Russell. 2016. *Managing ADHD in School: The Best Evidence-Based Methods for Teachers.* Eau Claire, WI: PESI Publishing and Media.

Greene, Ross W. 2014. *Lost at School: Why Our Kids with Behavioral Challenges Are Falling through the Cracks and How We Can Help Them.* New York: Scribner.

Reif, Sandra F. 2005. *How to Reach and Teach Children with ADD/ADHD: Practical Techniques, Strategies, and Interventions.* 2nd ed. San Francisco, CA: Jossey-Bass.

Autism and Sensory

Abraham, Dayna, Claire Heffron, Pamela Braley, and Lauren Drobnjak. 2015. *Sensory Processing 101.* Naperville, IL: LLA Media.

Attwood, Tony. 2008. *The Complete Guide to Asperger's Syndrome.* Philadelphia, PA: Jessica Kingsley.

Baker, Jed. 2001. *The Social Skills Picture Book: Teaching Play, Emotion, and Communication to Children with Autism.* Arlington, TX: Future Horizons.

Grandin, Temple. 2006. *Thinking in Pictures: My Life with Autism.* New York: Vintage Books.

Grandin, Temple. 2014. *The Autistic Brain: Helping Different Kinds of Minds Succeed.* Boston, MA: Mariner Books.

Kranowitz, Carol. 2022. *The Out-of-Sync Child: Recognizing and Coping with Sensory Processing Differences.* 3rd ed. New York: TarcherPerigee.

Sousa, David A., and Carol A. Tomlinson. 2018. *Differentiation and the Brain: How Neuroscience Supports the Learner-Friendly Classroom.* Moorabbin, Vic: Hawker Brownlow Education.

Watts, Mandisa. 2020. *Exciting Sensory Bins for Curious Kids: 60 Easy, Creative Play Projects that Boost Brain Development, Calm Anxiety, and Build Fine Motor Skills.* Salem, MA: Page Street Publishing.

Cerebral Palsy

Draper, Sharon M. 2012. *Out of My Mind.* New York: Atheneum Books for Young Readers.

A story about a girl with cerebral palsy. Written at the fourth-grade level but may also be interesting for teachers to read.

Dyslexia and Dysgraphia

David, Ronald. 2010. *The Gift of Dyslexia: Why Some of the Smartest People Can't Read . . . and How They Can Learn.* Rev. ed. New York: Perigee Books.

Dotterer, Cheri L. 2018. *Handwriting Brain-Body Disconnect: Adaptive Teaching Techniques to Unlock a Child's Dysgraphia for the Classroom and at Home.* Powell, OH: Author Academy Elite.

Olsen, Jan Z., Marcy Marxer, and Cathy Fink. 2003. *Handwriting without Tears.* Cabin John, MD: Handwriting Without Tears.

A multisensory handwriting program.

Rief, Sandra F., and Judith M. Stern. 2010. *The Dyslexia Checklist: A Practical Reference for Parents and Teachers.* San Francisco, CA: Jossey-Bass.

Shaywitz, Sally, and Jonathan Shaywitz. 2020. *Overcoming Dyslexia.* 2nd ed. New York: Vintage Books.

English Language Learners

Peregoy, Suzanne F., and Owen F. Boyle. 2016. *Reading, Writing, and Learning in ESL: A Resource Book for Teaching K–12 English Learners.* 7th ed. Boston, MA: Pearson.

Vernon, Shelley Ann. 2018. *176 English Language Games for Children Ages 6 to 12.* 5th ed. Scotts Valley, CA: CreateSpace.

Gifted Students

Galbraith, Judy, and Jim Delisle. 2015. *When Gifted Kids Do Not Have All the Answers: How to Meet Their Social and Emotional Needs.* 2nd ed. Huntington Beach, CA: Free Spirit.

Winebrenner, Susan, and Dina Brulles. 2018. *Teaching Gifted Kids in Today's Classroom: Strategies and Techniques Every Teacher Can Use.* 4th ed. Huntington Beach, CA: Free Spirit.

Appendix E:
Books for Children on Learning Variabilities

Andreae, Giles, and Guy Parker-Rees. 2001. *Giraffes Can't Dance.* New York: Scholastic.
All the animals can dance except the giraffe, until he learns to dance to his own beat. (Ages 1–5)

Antrobus, Raymond. 2022. *Can Bears Ski?* London, UK: Walker Books.
A sweet book about a bear with a hearing impairment. (Ages 3–7)

Backman, Laura. 2009. *Lemon the Duck.* Montréal: Lobster Press.
Lemon the Duck cannot walk, so the children work together to help. (Ages 3–6)

Bailey, Jenn. 2019. *A Friend for Henry.* San Francisco, CA: Chronicle Books.
About a young boy with autism, told from his point of view. (Ages 3–6)

Brakenhoff, Kelly. 2019. *Never Mind!* Lincoln, NE: Emerald Prairie Press.
Duke is a deaf dog who does not like it when he is told, "Never mind!" (Ages 3–8)

Brown, Keah. 2022. *Sam's Super Seats.* New York: Penguin Young Readers.
Young girl with cerebral palsy goes back-to-school shopping with her best friends. (Ages 3–8)

Carey, Becky. 2015. *47 Strings: Tessa's Special Code.* Mineral Point, WI: Little Creek Press.
A book about a child with Down syndrome. (Ages 8–12)

Clay, Kathryn. 2014. *Time to Sign: Sign Language for Kids.* North Mankato, MN: Capstone Press.
Teaches American Sign Language to use at home, at school, and in the community. (Ages 5–8)

Cook, Julia. 2018. *Uniquely Wired: A Story about Autism and Its Gifts.* Boys Town, NE: Boys Town Press.
Story told from the perspective of a boy with autism. (Ages 5–11)

Cotterill, Samantha. 2019. *This Beach Is Loud.* New York: Dial Books.
About a child at the beach who has sensory issues. (Ages 3–7)

Deak, JoAnn. 2010. *Your Fantastic Elastic Brain: Stretch It, Shape It.* Naperville, IL: Little Pickle Press.
Book tells how a person's brain can learn from mistakes, encourages a growth mindset. (Ages 4–8)

Demuth, Patricia B. 2020. *Who Is Temple Grandin?* New York: Penguin Random House.
A chapter book about Temple Grandin, famous for having autism and for developing better conditions for cattle. (Ages 8–12)

Flood, Nancy Bo. 2020. *I Will Dance.* New York: Atheneum Books for Young Readers.
A book about a girl in a wheelchair who wants to dance. (Ages 4–8)

Hudson, Katy. 2021. *Mindful Mr. Sloth.* North Mankato, MN: Capstone Editions.
A story of a girl who likes to go fast and a sloth who teaches her to slow down and enjoy everything around her. (Ages 5–8)

Jones, Jennifer. 2021. *Sensory Seeking Sloth.* Columbia, SC: J. Jones.
A story about a sloth that uses a sensory diet to calm down. (Ages 1–8)

Kensky, Jessica, and Patrick Downes. 2018. *Rescue and Jessica: A Life-Changing Friendship.* Somerville, MA: Candlewick Press.
A book about a young woman who has had a leg amputated, and her service dog. (Ages 5–8)

Lee, Britney Winn. 2019. *The Boy with Big, Big Feelings.* Minneapolis, MN: Beaming Books.
A boy with autism learns to cope in healthy ways with his feelings. (Ages 3–7)

Leipholtz, Beth. 2023. *The ABCs of Inclusion: A Disability Inclusion Book for Kids.*
Minneapolis, MN: Wise Ink.
This book teaches children that differences are not scary. (Ages 5–8)

Ludwig, Trudy. 2013. *The Invisible Boy.* New York: Alfred A. Knopf.
A story that teaches how small acts of kindness can help children feel included.
(Ages 5–8)

Maguire, Natalia. 2020. *My Body Sends a Signal: Helping Kids Recognise Emotions and
Express Feelings.* Hamburg, Germany: Maguire Books.
Addresses how children can learn to recognize and name their feelings and express
them in healthy ways. (Ages 3–7)

Meltzer, Brad. 2015. *I Am Helen Keller.* New York: Dial Books for Young Readers.
Helen Keller was blind and deaf, but she graduated from college, wrote books, and
was an advocate for people with disabilities. (Ages 5–9)

Millman, Isaac. 2002. *Moses Goes to a Concert.* New York: Farrar, Straus and Giroux.
A deaf child goes to a concert and is able to feel the vibrations from the drums.
Includes American Sign Language. (Ages 5–8)

Mosca, Julia Finley, and Daniel Rieley. 2018. *The Girl Who Thought in Pictures: The Story of
Dr. Temple Grandin.* New York: Scholastic.
Temple Grandin has autism, and no one expected her to be able to talk. She went on
to become a scientist. (Ages 4–9)

Newson, Karl, and Kate Hindley. 2019. *The Same but Different Too.* London, UK: Nosy Crow.
Addresses similarities and differences in positive ways. (Ages 2–6)

Parker, Lindsey Rowe. 2021. *Wiggles, Stomps, and Squeezes Calm My Jitters Down.*
Waynesville, NC: Boutique of Quality Books.
A book about sensory differences. (Ages 4–6)

Pimentel, Annette B. 2020. *All the Way to the Top: How One Girl's Fight for Americans with
Disabilities Changed Everything.* Naperville, IL: Sourcebooks.
An inspiring book about a girl in a wheelchair who pushed for changes. (Ages 5–9)

Polacco, Patricia. 2012. *Thank You, Mr. Falker.* New York: Philomel Books.
A teacher helps a girl struggling with dyslexia to learn to read. (Ages 6–10)

Rudolph, Shaina, and Danielle Royer. 2015. *All My Stripes: A Story for Children with Autism.*
Washington, DC: Magination Press.
A story about a zebra with autism who learns to appreciate himself for who he is.
(Ages 3-6)

Stocker, Shannon, and Devon Holzwarth. 2022. *Listen: How Evelyn Glennie, a Deaf Girl,
Changed Percussion.* New York: Dial Books for Young Readers.
A girl who loses her hearing discovers a new way to experience drums. (Ages 4–8)

Thomson, Gare. 2003. *Who Was Helen Keller?* New York: Penguin.
A chapter book about Hellen Keller, famous for being both blind and deaf and for
going on to graduate from college and becoming an author and activist. (Ages 7–10)

Thompson, Laurie Ann. 2015. *Emmanuel's Dream: The True Story of Emmanuel Ofosu
Yeboah.* Toronto: Anne Schwartz Books.
A true story about a boy born with a deformed leg and all that he was able to
accomplish. The message is that disability is not inability. (Ages 5–9)

Winkler, Henry, and Lin Oliver. 2014. *Bookmarks Are People Too!* Here's Hank series. New York: Penguin Workshop.

Winkler, Henry, and Lin Oliver. 2014. *A Short Tale about a Long Dog.* Here's Hank series. New York: Penguin Workshop.

Winkler, Henry, and Lin Oliver. 2014. *Stop That Frog!* Here's Hank series. New York: Penguin Workshop.
The Here's Hank series is a group of chapter books about children with learning differences. (Ages 6–8)

REFERENCES AND RECOMMENDED READING

20 USC 1400. 2004. Individuals with Disabilities Education Improvement Act of 2004.

Armstrong, Patricia. 1970. "Bloom's Taxonomy." Vanderbilt University. June 10. https://cft.vanderbilt.edu/guides-sub-pages/blooms-taxonomy/

Attwood, Tony. 2015. *The Complete Guide to Asperger's Syndrome.* Rev. ed. Philadelphia, PA: Jessica Kingsley Publishers.

AWE Learning. 2016. "Authentic Learning: Real-World Scenarios for Young Learners." Blog. AWE Learning. November 10. https://awelearning.com/blog/authentic-learning-young-learners/

Barber, Barry. 2012. "What the 4 C's: Communication, Collaboration, Creativity, and Critical Thinking Look Like in the Classroom." Collaborative Conference for Student Achievement: Engaging North Carolina in Transforming 21st Century Teaching and Learning. https://www.slideshare.net/barryrbarber/what-the-4-cs-communication-collaboration-creativity-and-critical-thinking-look-like-in-the-classroom-12095381

Boser, Katharina I., Matthew S. Goodwin, and Sarah C. Wayland. 2014. *Technology Tools for Students with Autism: Innovations that Enhance Independence and Learning.* Baltimore, MD: Paul H. Brookes Publishing.

Bowe, Frank G. 2000. *Universal Design in Education: Teaching Nontraditional Students.* Westport, CT: Bergin and Garvey.

Brookhart, Susan M. 2013. *How to Create and Use Rubrics for Formative Assessment and Grading.* Alexandria, VA: ASCD.

Bugaj, Christopher R. 2018. *The New Assistive Tech: Making Learning Awesome for All!* Arlington, VA: International Society for Technology in Education.

Burns, Monica, and Naomi Church. 2021. "How to Use Digital Math Tools with Your Students." Easy EdTech Podcast. May 4. https://uk01.l.antigena.com/l/lrUuZ XdmZLKHWpCNWc23J1QZgSvxQL1HY3ukfPFmf0QdqB-74YoUXhTw7gH_ fHU4WgToASsNbZGC9IJ0hnlqjgqvhk-5Kr2SgYAA~AGCcBPuar8GIXWYFgb9xWLw FxWj_Cl9GfpruZBu7VYaDfLF-SOxz7fOaS~VmLvwpHPsrJFl9vXtPQktfLd

Campbell, Nicci. 2011. "Supporting Children with Auditory Processing Disorder." *British Journal of Child Health* 6(6): 273–277.

CAST. 2018a. "The UDL Guidelines." Version 2.2. Wakefield, MA: CAST. http://udlguidelines.cast.org

CAST. 2018b. "UDL and the Learning Brain—CAST." Wakefield, MA: CAST. http://www.cast.org/products-services/resources/2018/udl-learning-brain-neuroscience

CAST. 2022a. "5 Examples of Universal Design for Learning in the Classroom." Understood. https://www.understood.org/en/articles/5-examples-of-universal-design-for-learning-in-the-classroom

CAST. 2022b. "The UDL Guidelines." Wakefield, MA: CAST. https://udlguidelines.cast.org/

Centers for Disease Control and Prevention. 2020a. "What Is Muscular Dystrophy?" CDC. https://www.cdc.gov/ncbddd/musculardystrophy/facts.html

Centers for Disease Control and Prevention. 2020b. "What Is Spina Bifida?" CDC. https://www.cdc.gov/ncbddd/spinabifida/facts.html

Centers for Disease Control and Prevention. 2022a. "Data and Statistics on Autism Spectrum Disorder." CDC. https://www.cdc.gov/ncbddd/autism/data.html

Centers for Disease Control and Prevention. 2022b. "Important Milestones: Your Baby by Three Years." Centers for Disease Control and Prevention. December 13. https://www.cdc.gov/ncbddd/actearly/milestones/milestones-3yr.html

Centers for Disease Control and Prevention. 2022c. "What Is ADHD?" CDC. https://www.cdc.gov/ncbddd/adhd/facts.html

Conn-Powers, Michael, Alice F. Cross, Elizabeth K. Traub, and Lois Hutter-Pishgahi. 2006. "The Universal Design of Early Education: Moving Forward for All Children." Young Children: Beyond the Journal. https://fpg.unc.edu/sites/fpg.unc.edu/files/resources/presentations-and-webinars/ConnPowersBTJ%281%29.pdf

Croft, Cindy. 2017. *Caring for Young Children with Special Needs.* St. Paul, MN: Redleaf Press.

Crouse, Stacy. 2019. "Classroom Accommodations for Children with Hearing Loss." StacyCrouse.com. https://www.stacycrouse.com/post/classroom-accommodations-for-children-with-hearing-loss

Dale, Naomi, Alison Salt, Jenefer Sargent, and Rebecca Greenaway, eds. 2022. *Children with Vision Impairment: Assessment, Development, and Management.* London, UK: Mac Keith Press.

Department of Children and Families. 2022. "What Is Early Childhood Inclusion?" *What Is Early Childhood Inclusion?* Wisconsin Department of Children and Families. https://dcf.wisconsin.gov/youngstar/eci/about#:~:text=The%20desired%20results%20of%20inclusive,to%20reach%20their%20full%20potential

Dodd, Sandra. 2019. *Sandra Dodd's Big Book of Unschooling.* 2nd ed. Erin, Ontario: Forever Curious Press.

Duncan, Sandra, Jody Martin, and Sally Haughey. 2018. *Through a Child's Eyes: How Classroom Design Inspires Learning and Wonder.* Lewisville, NC: Gryphon House.

Dunn, Rita, and Kenneth Dunn. 1975. "Learning Styles, Teaching Styles." *NASSP Bulletin* 59(393): 37–49.

Education Technology Solutions. 2018. "How Does Classroom Design Affect a Child's Ability to Learn?" Education Technology Solutions. https://educationtechnologysolutions.com/2018/04/classroom-design-affect-childs-ability-learn-14-medical-educational-experts-weigh/#:~:text=Flexible%20classroom%20designs%20allow%20learners,to%20different%20students'%20learning%20needs

Faber Taylor, Andrea, and Frances E. Kuo. 2011. "Could Exposure to Everyday Green Spaces Help Treat ADHD? Evidence from Children's Play Settings." *Applied Psychology: Health and Well-Being* 3 (3): 281–303. doi:10.1111/j.1758-0854.2011.01052.x

Fox, Kirsten. 2016. "Young Voice, Big Impact." *Principal* (November/December): 28–31. https://www.naesp.org/sites/default/files/Fox_ND16.pdf

Frauenberger, Christopher. 2015. "Rethinking Autism and Technology." *Interactions* 22(2): 57–59.

Gainsley, Suzanne. 2012. "Look, Listen, Touch, Feel, Taste: The Importance of Sensory Play." *HighScope Extensions* 25(5).

Gargot, Thomas, et al. 2020. "Acquisition of Handwriting in Children with and without Dysgraphia: A Computational Approach." *PLOS ONE* 15(9): e0237575. doi:10.1371/journal.pone.0237575

Gawrilow, Caterina, et al. 2013. "Physical Activity, Affect, and Cognition in Children with Symptoms of ADHD." *Journal of Attention Disorders* 20(2): 151–162.

Geneux, Valérie. 2021. "Our Brains Have a 'Fingerprint' Too." *ScienceDaily.* October 15. https://www.sciencedaily.com/releases/2021/10/211015184254.htm

Glaser, Marti. 2022. "How Technology Transformed the Classroom Experience for a Little Girl Living with a Genetic Neuromuscular Disease." NewsBreak. Spectrum News. January 25. https://www.newsbreak.com/news/2495557174570/how-technology-transformed-the-classroom-experience-for-a-little-girl-living-with-a-genetic-neuromuscular-disease.

Grandin, Temple, and Richard Panek. 2013. *The Autistic Brain: Thinking across the Spectrum.* Boston, MA: Houghton Mifflin Harcourt.

Grandin, Temple, and Oliver Sacks. 2006. *Thinking in Pictures.* 2nd ed. New York: Random House.

Granone, Francesca, and Elin Kirsti Lie Reikerås. 2021. "Preschoolers Learning by Playing with Technology." In *Education in Childhood.* London, UK: IntechOpen.

Griffiths, Timothy D. 2002. "Central Auditory Processing Disorders." *Current Opinion in Neurology* 15(1): 31–33.

Hall, Tracey E., Anne Meyer, and David H. Rose, eds. 2012. *Universal Design for Learning in the Classroom: Practical Applications.* New York: Guilford Press.

Hecker, Linda, et al. 2002. "Benefits of Assistive Reading Software for Students with Attention Disorders." *Annals of Dyslexia* 52(1): 243–272.

Higgins, Steven, et al. 2005. *The Impact of School Environments: A Literature Review.* The Centre for Learning and Teaching, School of Education, Communication, and Language Science. Newcastle upon Tyne, UK: Newcastle University.

Hinton, Denise, and Susan Kirk. 2014. "Teachers' Perspectives Of Supporting Pupils With Long-Term Health Conditions in Mainstream Schools: A Narrative Review Of The Literature." *Health and Social Care in the Community* 23(2): 107–120.

History Computer Staff. 2021. "Modern Computer Keyboard: Everything You Need to Know." History-Computer.com. https://history-computer.com/modern-computer-keyboard/

Hitchcock, Chuck, Anne Meyer, David Rose, and Richard Jackson. 2002. "Providing New Access to the General Curriculum." *Teaching Exceptional Children* 35(2): 8–17.

Hollingshead, Aleksandra, Joy Zabala, and Janice Carson. 2022. "The SETT Framework and Evaluating Assistive Technology Remotely." Council for Exceptional Children. https://exceptionalchildren.org/blog/sett-framework-and-evaluating-assistive-technology-remotely

Hughes, Julie. 2006. "Inclusive Education for Individuals with Down Syndrome." *Down Syndrome News and Update* 6(1): 1–3.

Hunt, Paula Frederica. 2021. "Inclusive Education: The Case for Early Identification and Early Intervention in Assistive Technology." *Assistive Technology* 33(supp.): S94–S101.

Ileto, Olivia S. 2019. "Emergent Technology as a Tool in Enhancing the Teaching Learning Process: An Assessment." *International Journal of Research Studies in Education* 8(4): 1–9.

Institute of Education Sciences, National Center For Education Statistics. n.d. "Determining Your Technology Needs." National Center for Education Statistics. https://nces.ed.gov/pubs2005/tech_suite/part_2.asp

International Dyslexia Association. 2002. "Definition of Dyslexia." International Dyslexia Association. https://dyslexiaida.org/definition-of-dyslexia/

Irwin, Clare. 2017. "Establishing Shared Terminology: Commonly Used Terms for English Learners." Yale School of Medicine. https://medicine.yale.edu/news-article/establishing-shared-terminology-commonly-used-terms-for-english-learners/#:~:text=While%20the%20terms%20DLL%20and,enter%20the%20K%2D12%20system

Jones, Keith. 2022. "Why We Educate: Equity in Education for All." Presentation. Virtual UDL Conference July 27–29.

Jordan, Adrian. 2022. "Why Is Student Voice Important in Education?" *Move This World.* November 23. https://www.movethisworld.com/classroom-resources/why-is-student-voice-important-in-education/#:~:text=Student%20voice%20is%20important%20for,stand%20up%20for%20a%20friend

Kaplan Early Learning Company. n.d. "Challenging Gifted Students in the Classroom." Blog. Kaplan Early Learning Company. https://www.kaplanco.com/ii/challenging-gifted-students-in-the-classroom

Kessler, David. 2020. *Finding Meaning: The Sixth Stage of Grief.* New York: Scribner.

Ladd, Helen F. 2012. "Education and Poverty: Confronting the Evidence." *Journal of Policy Analysis and Management* 31(2): 203–227.

Lee, Sean S. 2009. *Breath: Causes, Diagnosis, and Treatment of Oral Malodor.* 2nd ed. San Bernardino, CA: Culminare, Inc.

Mandell, Susan, Dennis H. Sorge, and James D. Russell. 2008. "Tips For Technology Integration." *Techtrends* 46(5): 39–43. doi:10.1007/bf02818307

Marfan Foundation. 2022. "What Are the Signs of Marfan Syndrome?" Marfan Foundation. https://marfan.org/expectations/signs/

McClaskey, Kathleen. 2022. "What Is Learner Variability and Why Does It Matter?" Empower the Learner. March 27. https://empowerthelearner.com/what-is-learner-variability-and-why-does-it-matter/

McLennan, Deanna Pecaski. 2014. "Making Math Meaningful for Young Children." *Teaching Young Children* 8(1).

McPherson, Donnesa. 2022. "What Assistive Technology for Speech and Language Disorders Are Available and How Do They Work?" *Autism Parenting Magazine* https://www.autismparentingmagazine.com/assistive-technology-speech-language-disorders

Merriam-Webster.com. 2022. "Poverty." Merriam-Webster.com Dictionary. https://www.merriam-webster.com/dictionary/poverty

Nash, Beth Ellen. 2017. *Dyslexia Outside-The-Box: Equipping Dyslexic Kids to Not Just Survive but Thrive.* York, PA: Transformation Books.

National Association for Down Syndrome. 2018. "Facts about Down Syndrome." NADS. https://www.nads.org/resources/facts-about-down-syndrome/

National Association for Gifted Children. n.d. "What Is Giftedness?" National Association for Gifted Children. http://www.nagc.org/WhatisGiftedness.aspx

National Association of Special Education Teachers. 2022. "Introduction to Learning Disabilities." NASET. https://www.naset.org/publications/ld-report/introduction-to-learning-disabilities

National Center for Education Statistics. n.d. "Part 2: Determining Your Technology Needs." https://nces.ed.gov/pubs2005/tech_suite/part_2.asp

National Institute of Mental Health. 2022. "Autism Spectrum Disorder." National Institutes of Health, National Institute of Mental Health. https://www.nimh.nih.gov/health/topics/autism-spectrum-disorders-asd

National Institute of Neurological Disorders and Stroke. 2022. "Dysgraphia." National Institute of Neurological Disorders and Stroke. https://www.ninds.nih.gov/health-information/disorders/dysgraphia

Nelson, Loui Lord. 2021. *Design and Deliver: Planning and Teaching Using Universal Design for Learning.* 2nd ed. Baltimore, MD: Paul H. Brookes Publishing.

Novak, Katie. 2016. *UDL Now! A Teacher's Guide to Applying Universal Design for Learning.* 2nd ed. Wakefield, MA: CAST Professional Publishing.

O'Neill, Jan, Anne Conzemius, Carol Commodore, and Carol Pulsfus. 2006. *The Power of SMART Goals: Using Goals to Improve Student Learning.* Bloomington, IN: Solution Tree Press.

O'Neill, Lucinda M. 2000. "Moving Toward the Vision of the Universally Designed Classroom." *The Exceptional Parent* 31(6): 31–33.

O'Neill, Lucinda M., and Bridget Dalton. 2002. "Supporting Beginning Reading in Children with Cognitive Disability through Technology." *The Exceptional Parent* 32(6): 40–43.

Ostertag, Curtis, et al. 2021. "Altered Gray Matter Development in Pre-Reading Children with a Family History of Reading Disorder." *Developmental Science* 25(2): e13160.

Painter, Helen. 2013. *Dysgraphia: Your Essential Guide.* Clarks Green, PA: HGP Industries.

Parker, Frieda, Jodie Novak, and Tonya Bartell. 2017. "To Engage Students, Give Them Meaningful Choices in the Classroom." *Phi Delta Kappan* 99(2): 37–41.

Pape, Barbara. 2018. Learner Variability Is the Rule, Not the Exception. https://digitalpromise.org/wp-content/uploads/2018/06/Learner-Variability-Is-The-Rule.pdf

Pisha, Bart, and Peggy Coyne. 2001. "Smart from the Start: The Promise of Universal Design for Learning." *Remedial and Special Education* 22(4): 197–203.

Planbook. 2022. "Flexible Classroom Design: How to Create a Student-Centered Learning Environment." Blog. Planbook. https://blog.planbook.com/flexible-classroom-design/

Polacco, Patricia. 2012. *Thank You, Mr. Falker.* New York: Philomel Books.

Powers, Julie. 2016. *Parent Engagement in Early Learning: Strategies for Working with Families.* 2nd ed. St. Paul, MN: Redleaf Press.

Puentedura, Ruben R. 2014. SAMR in the Classroom: Developing Sustainable Practice. http://www.hippasus.com/rrpweblog/archives/2014/11/28/SAMRInTheClassroom_DevelopingSustainablePractice.pdf

Quebec Education Program, Preschool Education. 2021. *Classroom Organization.* Quebec Ministry of Education. http://www.education.gouv.qc.ca/fileadmin/site_web/documents/education/jeunes/pfeq/Organization-preschool.pdf

Rappolt-Schlichtmann, Gabrielle, and Samantha G. Daley. 2013. "Providing Access to Engagement in Learning: The Potential of Universal Design for Learning in Museum Design." *Curator: The Museum Journal* 56(3): 307–321.

Rose, David H., and R. P. Dolan. 2000. "Universal Design for Learning." *Journal of Special Education Technology* 15(4): 47–51.

Rose, David H., and Anne Meyer. 2002. *Teaching Every Student in the Digital Age: Universal Design for Learning.* Alexandria, VA: ASCD.

Rose, David H., Sheela Sethuraman, and Grace J. Meo. 2000. "Universal Design for Learning." *Journal of Special Education and Technology* 15(2): 26–60.

Rose, Todd. 2013. "The Myth of Average: Todd Rose at TEDx Sonoma County." TEDxTalk. https://www.youtube.com/watch?v=4eBmyttcfU4

Roskos, Kathleen, and Susan B. Neuman. 2011. "The Classroom Environment." *The Reading Teacher* 65(2): 110–114.

Salus University Occupational Therapy Institute. 2021. "Six Developmental Benefits of Sensory Bins." Salus University Health. https://www.salusuhealth.com/Occupational-Therapy-Institute/Resources/News-Events/News-Stories/Six-Developmental-Benefits-of-Sensory-Bins.aspx

Seel, Norbert M., Marilla Svinicki, and Jane Vogler. 2012. "Motivation and Learning: Modern Theories." In *Encyclopedia of the Sciences of Learning.* New York, NY: Springer.

Sefton, Katie, Richard M. Gargiulo, and Stephen B. Graves. 1991. "Working with Families of Children with Special Needs." *Day Care and Early Education* 18(3): 40.

Shabiralyani, Ghulam, et al. 2015. "Impact of Visual Aids in Enhancing the Learning Process Case Research: District Dera Ghazi Khan." *Journal of Education and Practice* 6(19): 226–234.

Simon, Fran, and Karen N. Nemeth. 2012. *Digital Decisions: Choosing the Right Technology Tools for Early Childhood Education.* Lewisville, NC: Gryphon House.

Snelling, Jennifer. 2021. "Focus on UDL When Using Classroom Technology." ISTE. https://www.iste.org/explore/classroom/focus-udl-when-using-classroom-technology

Terada, Youki. 2020. "A Powerful Model for Understanding Good Tech Integration." Edutopia. https://www.edutopia.org/article/powerful-model-understanding-good-tech-integration

Thoma, Colleen A., Christina C. Bartholomew, and LaRon A. Scott. 2009. *Universal Design for Transition: A Roadmap for Planning and Instruction.* Baltimore, MD: Paul H. Brookes Publishing.

Tijnagel-Schoenaker, Bernadet. 2018. "The Reggio Emilia Approach . . . The Hundred Languages." *Prima Educatione* 1: 139. doi:10.17951/pe.2017.1.139

Tracy, Mary Teresa. 2019. "3 Tips for Organizing Preschool Classrooms." Region 13 Education Service Center. Blog. October 17. https://blog.esc13.net/3-tips-for-organizing-preschool-classrooms/

Thornburgh, Dick, and David R. Fine. 2000. "Pausing to Reflect on the ADA after 10 Years." *The Exceptional Parent* 58(72): 58–60.

Trudel, Heidi. 2007. "Making Data-Driven Decisions: Silent Reading." *The Reading Teacher* 61(4): 308–315.

Voss, Catalin, et al. 2019. "Effect of Wearable Digital Intervention for Improving Socialization in Children with Autism Spectrum Disorder: A Randomized Clinical Trial." *JAMA Pediatrics* 173(5): 446–454.

Vuchic, Vic, and Barbara Pape. 2018. "Understanding Learner Variability to Personalize Learning - Edsurge News." EdSurge. December 27. https://www.edsurge.com/news/2018-10-07-understanding-learner-variability-to-personalize-learning

Wood, J. 2001. "Every Kid Can!" *Instructor* 110(7): 63–74.

Zhang, Ling, et al. 2021. "Codesigning Learning Environments Guided by the Framework of Universal Design for Learning: A Case Study." *Learning Environments Research* 25(2): 379–397.

Zimmerman, Maya. 2022. "Parent Input on Having a Special Needs Child." Interview by Cindy Mudroch.

Zorzi, Marco, et al. 2012. "Extra-Large Letter Spacing Improves Reading in Dyslexia." *Proceedings of the National Academy of Sciences* 109(28): 11455–11459.

Index